A grammar of the modern Armenian language as spoken in Constantinople and Asia Minor

Elias Riggs

A

GRAMMAR

OF THE

MODERN ARMENIAN LANGUAGE

AS SPOKEN

IN CONSTANTINOPLE AND ASIA MINOR

By ELIAS RIGGS,
Missionary of the A. B. C. F. M.

SECOND EDITION.

CONSTANTINOPLE,
PRINTED BY A. B. CHURCHILL.

1856.

TABLE OF CONTENTS

PREFACE.

The strongly marked individuality of the Armenian language justifies its claim to a very high antiquity. Its literature however commences with the introduction of Christianity. The Alphabet still in use is ascribed to St. Mesrob, who lived in the fifth century, and who was one of the translators of the Scriptures. He is said also to have conferred the boon of alphabetic writing upon several of the neighboring nations. The original alphabet consisted of thirty six letters, o and փ having been added during the twelfth century, the former as a substitute for the diphthong աւ in words where it had acquired the sound of *o*, and the latter to replace փ which had come to be pronounced universally like *p*.

It is difficult to trace the history of the modern language. Evidence of the existence of some of its distinctive forms is found as far back as the thirteenth century. Their introduction was no doubt gradual. Still the Ancient Armenian continued to be the only language of books, for ages after the spoken tongue had become substantially what it is at the present day. It is only during the present century that the modern language has begun to be cultivated as a language of books, the genius of the age and the best interests of humanity requiring that authors should no longer, as formerly, veil their ideas in a dialect accessible only to the few, but should spread them far and wide in the free and idiomatic use of the languages vernacular to their countrymen.

Facilities for the acquisition of the *Ancient* Armenian exist both in English and in other European tongues, and an abundance of excellent Grammars and Lexicons await the scholar, who is prepared to avail himself of them, in the language itself. But, so far as I am aware, the present is the first attempt to exhibit the grammar of the Modern Armenian. The Armenians themselves have, as yet, published no grammar of their spoken language*. This fact will no doubt be deemed a sufficient apology for any defects which may be discovered in the present work.

My principal object has been to exhibit the language of conversation. Hence the remarks on pronunciation, pp. 7, 58, on the reduplication of adjectives, p. 19, on particles appended to verbs, p. 49, &c. The style of books varies considerably, some approximating more and others less to the ancient language. It would be presumptuous to attempt to say what, after a few years of progress, will be the style of good writers.

It will be observed that the dialect here treated is the Western, viz. that spoken in Constantinople and Asia Minor. The Oriental dialect, spoken in Tartary, Persia and India, varies considerably from this, and in some respects approximates more nearly to the ancient language. A specimen of it will be given in the Appendix.

The student of Modern Armenian will very often meet in conversation, and sometimes even in books, with words and forms derived from the Turkish. Although the use of such words and forms is avoided by good writers, still a knowledge of them is essential to a familiar acquaintance with the spoken Armenian. Where it has been thought proper to notice them in the present work, they are distinguished by an asterisk prefixed.

In general, where two synonymous forms are given, the one more approved in modern usage is placed first.

_____

*The first edition of this work was published in 1847. In 1853 a grammatical treatise in Modern Armenian appeared at Constantinople, entitled "Correct Method of speaking the Modern Armenian language". It is however not so much a grammar of the spoken language, as an exhibition of the author's ideas of what that language should be, departing in many instances very far from existing usage. It has met with very little favor.

PART I.

ORTHOGRAPHY.

ALPHABET.

The Armenian alphabet consists of 38 letters, viz.

Capitals.	Arm. text.	Italics.	Names.	Pronunciation.
Ա	ա	*ա*	aip	a as in *far*
Բ	բ	*բ բ*	pen	p
Գ	գ գ	*գ գ*	kim	k
Դ	դ դ	*դ դ*	tah	t
Ե	ե	*ե*	yetch	ye as in *yet*, y
Զ	զ զ	*զ զ*	zah	z
Է	է	*է*	a	a as in *fate*
Ը	ը ը	*ը ը*	yet	u as in *us*
Թ	թ թ	*թ թ*	to	t
Ժ	ժ	*ժ*	zhay	s as in *pleasure*
Ի	ի ի	*ի ի*	inni	e as in *me*
Լ	լ լ	*լ լ*	lune	l
Խ	խ խ	*խ խ*	khay	kh guttural
Ծ	ծ	*ծ*	dzah	dz
Կ	կ կ	*կ կ*	ghen	g hard
Հ	հ	*հ*	ho	h
Ձ	ձ	*ձ*	tsah	ts
Ղ	ղ ղ	*ղ ղ*	ghad	gh guttural
Ճ	ճ	*ճ*	jay	j
Մ	մ	*մ*	men	m
Յ	յ	*յ*	he	h *or* y
Ն	ն	*ն*	noo	n
Շ	շ շ	*շ շ*	shah	sh
Ո	ո	*ո*	vo	vo *or* o

Ձ	ՀՀ	ՀՀ	chah	ch as in *church*
Ղ	Ղ	Ղ	bay	b
Ճ	ՃՃ	ՃՃ	chay	ch as in *church*
Մ	ս	—	rrah	r Scotch
Յ	ս	ս	say	s
Ն	ՆՆ	ՆՆ	vev	v
Շ	ս	ս	dune	d
Ո	Ո Ո	Ո Ո	ray	r
Չ	ց ց	ց ց	tso	ts
Պ	ս	—	hune	u *or* v
Ջ	փ փ	փ փ	pure	p
Ռ	ք ք	ք	kay	k
Ս	ո	ո	o	o
Վ	ֆ	ֆ	fay	f

Ⴑ is a contraction for *եւ*; beside which the following combinations of letters occur.

ս and ո	ՍՈ		ս and ս	ՍՍ	
ս and ե	ՍԵ		ս and ս	ՍՍ	
ս and է	ՍԷ		ս and ս	ՍՍ	
ս and ի	ՍԻ		ս and ս	ՍՍ	

The small letters at the right hand of the second and third columns are written *after* those which terminate in a horizontal stroke at the bottom: as ՍԵ, ՂԵ, ՆԵ, &c.

PRONUNCIATION.

Ե, when it begins a word and is followed by a consonant, is pronounced generally like *ye* in *yet*, as *եմ* yem *I am*; elsewhere followed by a consonant it is like *e* in *fell*, as *մենք* menk *we*; followed by a vowel it is simply *y*, as *եօթը* yotuh *seven*, *կեանք* gyank *life*.

Խ and ղ are deep gutturals, and the pronunciation of them must be acquired through the ear.

Յ is *h* in the beginning of words, as *Յիսուս* Hesoos *Jesus*; elsewhere it is *y*, as *այո* ayo *yes*, *կայարան* ga-yaran *a position*, *բայ* pay *a verb*; but in compound words in which the latter part is a word beginning with *յ*, this latter retains the sound of *h* in the compound, as *բացայայտ* patsahaid *manifest*, compounded of *բաց* open, and *յայտ* evident. At the end of words it is frequently silent, as *կայ* gah *there is*.

Ո is *vo* at the beginning of words, as *որ* vor *that*, except when followed by *վ* as *ով* ov *who*; elsewhere it is *օ*, as *անոնք* anonk *they*.— The combination *ու* is *oo*, but becomes *v* * before a vowel; *ոյ* in the middle of a word is *ooy* as in *լոյս* looys *light*, *յոյս* hooys *hope*; at the end of a word it is simply *o*.

Իւ is *eev* before a vowel or at the end of a word; elsewhere it is *u* in *unit*, or *u* French. In any other combination, *ւ* is *v*.

The remaining letters are uniform in their pronunciation, and need no remark.

When two or more consonants come together without a vowel, they are frequently pronounced as if written with *ը*; e. g. Սկրտիչ *Baptist* is pronounced *Մկրըտիչ*. In the case of words commencing with one of the sibilants *ս*, *զ*, or *շ* and another consonant, this euphonic *ը* is generally pronounced as if written *before* the sibilant, as *սկիզբէն* *from the beginning*, *զրուցանը* a-

---

* Soft like the German *w*.

musement, շտնմարան *magazine,* pronounced as if written
բակիզէն, բզրոստանք and բշտնմարան. This however is
not always the fact, and, in general, the place of this
euphonic ը must be learned by practice.

ACCENT.

Armenian words, whether primitive or derivative,
are usually accented on the last syllable.

Exc. 1. ը at the end of words not derived from
the Turkish cannot receive the accent. Words or
forms terminating in this vowel, therefore, accent the
penultimate ; as վաղը *to-morrow,* մարդը *the man.*

Exc. 2. Vocatives accent their first syllable ; as
Սարգապետ *Preacher !* Պարոն *Sir !* —But when a
noun in the Vocative is repeated, or is preceded by
an adjective or by the interjection Ո՛վ *O,* the place
of the accent is on the last syllable of the first
noun, or on the adjective or interjection, as Յակոբ
Յակոբ, Բարի վարդապետ, Ո՛վ Երրաչամ :

Exc. 3. A few individual words, not coming under
either of the above exceptions, accent the penultimate as հիմա *now,* այսպէս *thus.*

PUNCTUATION.

The pauses used in Armenian are three, viz.

Comma (,)
Colon (·)
Period (։)

The note of interrogation (՞) is placed over the

accented vowel of the principal word in the question. Accordingly in the question, *Will you come to-morrow ?* the interrogation point may be placed over any one of the words of which it is composed in Armenian ; thus, 'Ւուն վաղը կուգաս , signifies *Will you come to-morrow ?* 'Ւուն վաղը կուգաս , *Will you come to-morrow ?* 'Ւուն վաղը կուգաս , *Will* you come to-morrow ?

The exclamation point (′) in like manner, is placed over the accented syllable of interjections, or of other words used as exclamations, or uttered with emotion, as վայ *wo* ! Երուսաղէմ *Jerusalem* !

Sentences, which contain a mark of interrogation or exclamation, have still their appropriate pauses at the close, in the same way as other sentences.

The hyphen (ـ) is never employed to unite words, as in the English compounds *to-day, kettle-drum,* &c. Its only place is at the end of a line, where a word is incomplete.

The acute accent (′), though it is placed upon the tone-syllable of words, has for its object to mark rather *emphasis* than accent. Hence monosyllables receive it as well as polysyllables ; e. g. Մ երթար *do not go,* թէ հոս թէ հոն , *whether here or there.*

The grave accent (`) indicates a brief suspension of the voice. It is placed after words, never over them, and is in effect a pause shorter than a comma.

This mark (‾) indicates an abbreviation ; as, Ա՟ծ for Աստուած ; or signifies that the letters over which it is placed are used as figures ; e. g. ա̅ 1 , բ̅ 2 , &c.

When the first part of a word is written and the last part omitted, the omission is indicated by a double accent ; thus Յովհ՞ for Յովհաննէս :

PART II.

E T Y M O L O G Y.

ARTICLE.

The word in Modern Armenian which most nearly corresponds to our Indefinite Article is *մը* , a corruption of the Ancient Armenian *մի one.* It uniformly follows the noun to which it belongs ; as *մարդ մը a man, բան մը a thing.* The Numeral Adjective *մէկ one* is used in the same sense, preceding the noun. Sometimes both are employed ; as *մէկ մարդ մը , մէկ բան մը* , without any addition to the signification.

The place of a Definite Article is supplied by the *Definite Form* of nouns, corresponding to what is called the Emphatic State in Chaldee and Syriac.

N O U N S.

GENDER.

The Armenian language has no grammatical forms to mark the distinction of gender.

NUMBER.

The Plural Number is regularly formed by adding to monosyllables *եր* ; as *բառ , word, բառեր words;* to words of more than one syllable *ներ* ; as *հագուստ, garment, հագուստներ , garments.*

Though the singular have but one written vowel, yet if it is pronounced with a euphonic _ը_ it is a dissyllable, and takes _ներ_ to form the plural ; as _գլուխ_ head (pron. _գըլուխ_) Plur. _գլուխներ._

A Plural ending iu _ք_, like that of Ancient Armenian nouns, is occasionally employed, as _որդի_ son, _որդիք_ sons. See Appendix.

CASE.

Nouns in the modern language may be said to have seven _cases_, the Nominative, Genitive, Dative, Accusative, Vocative, Ablative and Instrumental. They present however in general only four distinct forms, the Accusative being (in nouns thugh not in pronouns) the same with the Nominative, and the Dative with the Genitive. The Vocative is distinguished from the Nominative by prefixing the interjection _Ո՛վ_ O, or by a change of the accent. See above on Accent, p. 9. The other three cases of the Ancient Armenian are supplied by the Genitive with Postpositions.

DEFINITE FORM.

The _Definite form_ of nouns is produced by adding _ը_ to the simple form when the latter ends with a consonant, and _ն_ when it ends with a vowel ; as _ժամ_ church, _ժամը_ the church, _որդի_ son, _որդին_ the son. The _ը_ of the definite form also becomes _ն_ when the following word begins with a vowel and is closely united in pronunciation with the noun ; as _մազերն ալ_ the hairs also, for _մազերը ալ_ .

DECLENSION OF NOUNS.

Բառ *a word*, is an example of the most usual mode of declining nouns which end with a consonant. The Definite form, of course, lacks the Vocative.

INDEFINITE FORM.

Singular.	*Plural.*
Nom· Բառ (մը) a word	Բառեր words
Gen· Բառի (մը) of a word	Բառերու of words
Dat· Բառի (մը) to *or* for a word	Բառերու to *or* for words
Acc· Բառ (մը) a word	Բառեր words
Voc Ով բառ O word	Ով բառեր O words
Abl· Բառէ (մը) from a word	Բառերէ from words
Inst· Բառով (մը) with a word	Բառերով with words

DEFINITE FORM.

Nom· Բառը the word	Բառերը the words
Gen· Բառին of the word	Բառերուն of the words
Dat· Բառին to *or* for the word	Բառերուն to *or* for the words
Acc· Բառը the word	Բառերը the words
Abl· Բառէն from the word	Բառերէն from the words
Inst· Բառով with the word	Բառերովը with the words

3

Example of a noun ending with a vowel.

INDEFINITE FORM.

Singular.   *Plural.*

Nom Որդի (Մր) a son   Որդիներ sons
Gen. Որդիի (Մր) of a son   Որդիներու of sons
Dat. Որդիի (Մր) to *or* for   Որդիներու to *or* for sons
    a son
Acc. Որդի (Մր) a son   Որդիներ sons
Voc. Ո՛րդի *or* Ո՛վ որդի O   Ո՛րդիներ *or* Ո՛վ որդիներ
    son   O sons
Abl. Որդիէ (Մր) from a   Որդիներէ from sons
    son
Inst. Որդիով (Մր) with a   Որդիներով with sons
    son

DEFINITE FORM.

Nom Որդին the son   Որդիները the sons
Gen. Որդիին of the son   Որդիներուն of the sons
Dat. Որդիին to *or* for the   Որդիներուն to *or* for the
    son   sons
Acc. Որդին the son   Որդիները the sons
Abl Որդիէն from the son   Որդիներէն from the sons
Inst. Որդիովը with the   Որդիներովը with the sons
    son

IRREGULAR NOUNS.

Nearly all the variations from the above forms, which appear in the declension of Nouns in Modern Armenian, are remnants of the Ancient Armenian declensions. The following are the principal.

To prevent ambiguity the prefix *զ* , which forms the Accusative in Ancient Armenian, is occasionally employed to distinguish that case from the Nominative ; as Ա՛ն Մարդը որ զԱստուած կը սիրէ *the man who loves God.* If written without the *զ* this sentence might be translated, *the man whom God loves.*

Nouns ending in *իւն* may be declined after the following paradigm.

Nom.	Ճ՛ամբորդութիւն	a journey
Gen	Ճ՛ամբորդութեան	
Dat	Ճ՛ամբորդութեան	
Acc.	Ճ՛ամբորդութիւն	
Voc.	Ա՛յ Ճամբորդութիւն	
Abl.	Ճ՛ամբորդութենէ	
Inst.	Ճ՛ամբորդութեամբ	

The plurals are regular, excepting that the ancient Genitive, ending in *եանց* , occasionally appears.

These nouns may also be declined throughout after the regular form, especially when used as proper names or in a peculiar sense ; e. g. we may translate the phrase *of the journey* Ճամբորդութիւնին or Ճամբորդութեանը , but if we are speaking of a book entitled Ճ՛ամբորդութիւնը the Gen. must be Ճ՛ամբորդութիւնին . So Յարութեան օրը *the day of the resurrection,* but Պ. Յարութիւնին գիրքը *Mr. Harootune's book ;* սրբութեան *of holiness,* սրբութիւնին *of the Sanctuary.*

Nouns which in Ancient Armenian terminate in *ումն* , in the modern language either retain the final *ն* and form the Gen. in *ման* , or drop that letter and are declined regularly ; thus օծումն *anointing,* Gen. օծման , or օծում , Gen. օծմի , The Inst. Sing. օծ_ ծամբ and the Nom. and Gen. Plur. օձմունք and օձ մանց, also occur

A few nouns, chiefly monosyllables, make the Gen· in ոյ instead of ի ; as մարգու ․ արջու ․ կովու ․ գիու ․ հովու ․ ծովու ․ սովու ․ զարու ․ &c ; but all these, ex cept the first, may take the regular form of the Gen. in ի .

Infinitives, when declined as nouns, uniformly make their Gen· in ոյ ; as գործել ․ գործելոյ . The other cases are regular.

Հայր *father,* has the Gen. & Dat· Sing· հօր , Abl. հօրէ or հօրմէ ․ Inst. հարբով ․ հայրով or հօրմով .

Like it are declined its derivatives ; also մայր *mo ther,* and եղբայր *brother* and their derivatives. The Plurals are regular

Աստուած *God,* Gen. & Dat. Աստուծոյ . Abl. Աստուծ մէ ․ Inst. Աստուծմով or Աստուծով .

Տէր *Lord,* Gen and Dat· Տեառն (in the title of the New Testament Տեառն) Abl Տեառնէ ․ Inst. Տեառն մով ․ Տեառմով , (or տիրոջ ․ տիրոջմէ ․ տիրոջմով).

Այր *man,* Gen and Dat· մարդու or մարդոյ. Nom. & Acc Plur. մարդիկ , Gen. & Dat. մարդոց. Abl. մար դոցմէ ․ Inst· մարդոցմով ; or մարդիկներ , մարդիկներու , մարդիկներէ ․ մարդիկներով .

Որդի *son,* besides being declined regularly, has the Gen· & Dat· Sing· (especially when applied to the Son of God) Որդւոյ ․ Plural որդիք ․ որդւոց ․ որդւոց մէ ․ որդւոցմով .

So եկեղեցի has sometimes եկեղեցւոյ , and հոգի հոգւոյ (especially when used for the Holy Spirit).

Աչք *eye,* ձեռք *hand,* and ոտք *foot* frequently form their Plurals, especially in the language of conversation, *աշուբներ ձեռուբներ* and *ոտուբներ*. But *աշբեր*, *ձեռբեր*, *ոտբեր*, should be preferred. Gen. Plur *աշաց*, *ձեռաց*, *ոտից*, or regularly *աշբերու*, *ձեռբերու*, *ոտբերու*.

Օր day, Gen. *օրին* *օրուան*, or *աւուր*, Abl. *օրունէ*.

Կին or կնիկ woman, wife, Gen. & Dat. *կնկան*, *կնոջ*, or *կնիկի*.

Երիկ husband, Gen. & Dat. *էրկան* or *էրիկի*.

Մանուկ child, *մանկան* or *մանուկի*.

Բուռ handful, *բռան* or *բուռի*.

Փուռ oven, *փռան* or *փուռի*.

Նուռ pomegranate, *նռան* or *նուռի*.

Դուռ door, *դրան* (with ʼ in the Gen. but preserving the ʼ in the other oblique cases) *դռնէ*, *դռնով*, or *դուռի*, *դուռէ*, *դուռով*.

Առտու morning, *առտուան*, *առտունէ*.

Իրիկուն evening, *իրիկուան*, *իրիկունէ*.

Գիշեր night, *գիշերուան* or *գիշերու*, *գիշերունէ*.

Տարի year, *տարուան* or *տարւոյ*, *տարունէ*.

Ամիս month, *ամսուան* or *ամսու*, *ամսունէ*.

Շաբաթ week, *շաբթուան* or *շաբթու*, *շաբթունէ*.

The last three are thus declined particularly when used to express duration; as *վեց ամսուան է* he is six months old; *անցած տարունէ մինչև հիմա* from last year till now; otherwise they are regular; as *տարիին վերջը* the end of the year, *վեցերորդ ամսին անունը փոխուեցաւ* the name of the sixth month was changed. The preceding three also may be declined regularly.

Որդայ a son, Gen. and Dat. *որդու*, Abl. *որդէ*, Inst. *որդով*, Plur. *որդայք* or *որդուքներ*, Gen. and Dat. *որդայոց* or *որդոց*, Abl. *որդոցմէ*, Inst. *որդոցմով*. It may also be declined regularly *որդայ*, *որդայի*, &c.

Մահ death, *մահու* or *մահուան*.

Ժողովուրդ *people,* ժողովրդեան.

Գլուխ *head,* գլխու, գլխէ, գլխով, Plur. գլխեր.

Գարուն *spring,* գարնան.

Աշուն *autumn,* աշնան.

Տուն *house,* տան, տնէ, տնով.

Քոյր (քուր, քոր) *sister,* քրոջ, քրոջմէ, քրոջմով.

Կեանք *life,* կենաց.

Երկինք *heaven,* երկնից.

Առաքեալ *Apostle,* առաքելոյ, Gen. Plur. առաքելոց.

But we may also say, ժողովուրդի, գլուխի, գարունի, աշունի, տունի, քոյրի, կեանքի, երկինքի, առաքեալի &c.

Proper names are for the most part declined regularly ; occasionally however they present an Ancient Armenian Genitive form in այ or ու ; as Ադամայ, Աբրահամու.

Nouns which have է in the last syllable of the Nominative sometimes change that vowel in the oblique cases of the Singular into ի ; as պարտէզ *a garden,* պարտէզի or պարտիզի ; վէճ *a dispute,* վէճի or վիճի ; sometimes (in proper names) into ե ; as Սիւքէմ, Gen. Սիւքեմի or Սիւքեմայ. If the last vowel of the Nom. be ի or ու it is sometimes dropped in the oblique cases ; as սիրտ, սրտի ; օգուտ, օգտի. The same occurs, though more rarely, with ա ; as քաղաք, քաղքի.

ADJECTIVES.

Adjectives, as in English, are undeclined, except when used as substantives.

COMPARISON OF ADJECTIVES.

The Comparative degree is formed by prefixing *աւելի more*, or it is the simple form of the Positive. In either case it takes an Ablative of the noun ; as *տունէն բարձր*, or *տունէն աւելի բարձր higher than the house.* Occasionally the ancient form of the comparative (terminating in *գոյն*) is met with, as *լաւագոյն better, մեծագոյն greater.*

The Superlative is formed from the Positive by prefixing *ամէն* (with *ա* for a union-vowel when the Adjective begins with a consonant), as *ամէնաբարի best, ամէնիմաստ wisest* ; or by a reduplication of the Positive, as *մեծամեծ greatest, very great, չարաչար very bad* ; or it is (like the Comparative) a simple Positive in the definite form construed with an Ablative of the noun as *ամէնէն մեծը the greatest of all.*

In the language of common conversation many adjectives admit a sort of *reduplication* which gives them the force of superlatives.

The syllable prefixed consists of the first consonant of the adjective, (if it begin with a consonant), the first vowel, and the letter *ի* or *ս*, more rarely *ր* or *մ*, according as euphony requires ; thus *լեցուն full, լեի լեցուն brim full, շիտակ straight, շիի շիտակ perfectly straight, մութ dark, մուս մութ very dark, pitch dark, մինակ alone, միս մինակ all alone, quite alone.* In like maner, *ճերի ճերմակ very white, երի երկան very long, թեի* (or *թեր*) **թեմիզ very clean, ծուի* (or *ծում*) *ծուռ very crooked,* &c.

The following forms are also a kind of Superlative, *պզտրտիկ very small,* from *պզտիկ small, մանրրտիկ very fine*, (spoken of powder, or any thing in grains) from մանր , a corruption of մանր *fine, small.*

The termination կեկ (occasionally կակ) gives to adjectives a diminutive signification ; e. g. թեթևկեկ *rather light,* ծանրկեկ *rather heavy,* մեծկակ *rather large.*

NUMERAL ADJECTIVES.

Cardinals.		Ordinals.	
1.	մէկ		առաջին
2.	երկու		երկորդ
3.	իրեք		երրորդ
4	չորս		չորրորդ
5	հինգ		հինգերորդ
6.	վեց		վեցերորդ
7.	եոթը		եոթներորդ
8.	ութը		ութերորդ
9.	ինը		իններորդ
10.	տասը		տասներորդ
11.	տասնումէկ		մետասաներորդ
12.	տասներկու		երկոտասաներորդ
13.	տամնիրեք		երեքտասաներորդ
14.	տասնուչորս		չորեքտասաներորդ
15.	տասնուհինգ		կզգետասաներորդ
16.	տասնուվեց		վեշտասաներորդ
17.	տասնուեոթը		եոթնուտասաներորդ
18.	տասնուութը		ութուտասաներորդ
19	տասնուինը		իններուտասաներորդ
20	քսան		քսաներորդ
21.	քսանումէկ		քսանումէկերորդ
22.	քսաներկու		քսաներկուերորդ
30.	երեսուն		երեսուներորդ

40.	քառասուն	քառասունևրորդ
50.	յիսուն	յիսունևրորդ
60.	վաթսուն	վաթսունևրորդ
70.	եօթանասուն	եօթանասունևրորդ
80.	ութսուն	ութսունևրորդ
90.	իննսուն	իննսունևրորդ
100.	հարիւր	հարիւրերորդ
200.	երկու հարիւր	երկու հարիւրերորդ
300.	իրեք հարիւր	իրեք հարիւրերորդ
1,000.	հազար	հազարերորդ
10,000.	բիւր or տասը հազար	տասը հազարերորդ

From 11 to 19 the ordinals are frequently formed from the cardinals by simply adding երորդ ; as տասն֊վեցերորդ sixteenth.

The cardinals are sometimes employed instead of ordinals ;   as Սաղմոս քսաներկու the twenty second Psalm.

Երկու without a substantive expressed becomes եր֊կուք . In like manner ամէն all, when its substantive is understood, becomes ամէնք .

Value of the letters of the alphabet used as numerals.

ա	1	ժ	10	ճ	100	ռ	1000
բ	2	ի	20	մ	200	ս	2000
գ	3	լ	30	յ	300	վ	3000
դ	4	խ	40	ն	400	տ	4000
ե	5	ծ	50	շ	500	ր	5000
զ	6	կ	60	ո	600	ց	6000
է	7	հ	70	չ	700	ւ	7000
ը	8	ձ	80	պ	800	փ	8000
թ	9	ղ	90	ջ	900	ք	9000

4

PRONOUNS.

Pronouns, as in other languages, are divided into Personal, Relative, Interrogative, Demonstrative, and Possessive. Like the Shemitic dialects, the Armenian has also pronominal suffixes.

The following is the declension of the *Personal* Pronouns. The Accusatives *all* take the prefix զ occasionally, but those of the first and second persons not commonly.

1. Ես *I.*

	Sing.	Plur.
Nom.	Ես I	Մեք we
Gen.	Իմ *or* իմին of me	Մեր *or* մերին of us
Dat.	Ինձ *or* ինծի to *or* for me	Մեզի *or* մեզ to *or* for us
Acc.	Իս *or* զիս me	Մեզ *or* զմեզ us
Abl.	Ինձմէ *or* ինէ from me	Մեզմէ *or* մենէ from us
Inst.	Ինձմով with me.	Մեզմով with us

2. Դուն *thou.*

Nom.	Դուն thou	Դուք ye
Gen.	Քու *or* քուկին of thee	Ձեր *or* ձերին of you
Dat.	Քեզի *or* քեզ to *or* for thee	Ձեզ *or* ձեզի to *or* for you
Acc.	Քեզ *or* զքեզ thee	Ձեզ *or* զձեզ you
Voc.	Ով դուն O thou	Ով դուք O ye
Abl.	Քեզմէ *or* քենէ from thee	Ձեզմէ *or* ձենէ from you
Inst.	Քեզմով with thee	Ձեզմով with you

3 Ինքր , *he, she, it.*

Nom.	Ինքր he, she, it	Իրենք they	
Gen.	Իր or իրեն of him, her, it	Իրենց of them	
Dat.	Իրեն to *or* for him, her, it	Իրենց to *or* for them	
Acc.	Ինքր *or* զինքր him, her, it	Իրենք *or* զիրենք them	
Abl.	Իրմէ from him, &c.	Իրենցմէ from them	
Inst.	Իրմով with him, &c.	Իրենցմով with them	

The Datives of the Personal Pronouns are occasionally used as Accusatives, and in like manner the Accusatives (without զ) as Datives ; as Ինծի ծեծեցին *They beat me*, Ըսի քեզ *I said to thee.*

The *Relative* որ *who, which*, is applied equally to persons and things. It is thus declined.

	Sing.	*Plur.*	
Nom.	Որ who, which	Որոնք who, which	
Gen.	Որու or որի of whom *or* of which	Որոնց of whom &c.	
Dat.	Որու or որի to whom *or* to which	Որոնց to whom, &c.	
Acc.	Որ or զոր whom *or* which	Որոնք or զորոնք	
Abl.	Որմէ from whom, &c.	Որոնցմէ from whom, &c.	
Inst.	Որմով with *or* by whom *or* which	Որոնցմով with *or* by whom &c.	

The *Interrogative* Pronouns are, for persons ով *who ?* for things ինչ *what ?* The former, which is both singular and plural, is not declined, but takes for its oblique cases those of *որ* ; as Որո՞ւ տուիր *to whom did you give ?* Որոնցմէ՞ առիր *from whom did you take ?* Ինչ is declined like the more usual form of nouns, except that the Genitive and Dative Sing. is ինչու , as well as ինչի.

The usual forms of the *Demonstrative* Pronouns are աս , աատ , and ան , though they occasionally appear with the ancient forms այս , այդ , and այն . The last may serve as an example of the way in which they are declined.

Ան , that, he, she, it.

Nom. Ան , անի , or Անիկայ that (person *or* thing.)   Անոնք those (persons or things)

Gen. & Dat. Անոր of or to that   Անոնց of *or* to those

Acc. Անի , անիկայ , զանի or զանիկայ that   Անոնք or զանոնք those

Abl. Անկէ , անկէց , անկից or անորմէ from that   Անոնցմէ from those

Inst. Անով with that   Անոնցմով with those

Աս *this* (rarely աս ,) and աատ *that* (but referring to an object less distant than ան) are declined in the same manner. When joined with nouns all three remain undeclined, like adjectives, as աս մարդուն *of this man,* ան բաները *those things.*

These three demonstrative pronouns are sometimes spoken of by the Armenians as *personal* ; ասա being regarded as of the first person, and as having a refe-rence to something near or connected with the

SUFFIX PRONOUNS.

speaker, *ատ* of the second, and relating to something near or connected with the person addressed. *Ա՛ն* is of the third person, of course.

There are two other forms of the these *Demonstrative* Pronouns in vulgar use ; viz. *սի*, *տի* and *նի* as adjectives, like *աս*, *ատ* and *ան* ; and *սրվի* or *սրվիկայ*, *տրվի* or *տրվիկայ*, ond *նրվի* or *նրվիկայ*, which are used without nouns and are declined thus.

	Sing.	Plur.
Nom & Acc.	Սրվի or սրվիկայ	Սրվոնք
Gen. & Dat.	Սրվոր	Սրվոնց
Abl.	Սրվորմէ, սրկէց or սրնկից	Սրվոնցմէ
Inst.	Սրվորմով or սրվով	Սրվոնցմով

The *Suffixes* are appended to nouns and particles, not to verbs. They are

For the Singular	For the Plur. without a noun or pronoun in the Gen. case preceding
1 pers. *ս*	1 pers. *երնիս* or *նիս*
2 pers. *դ*	2 pers. *երնիդ* or *նիդ*
3 pers. *ը* or *ն*	3 pers *երնին* or *նին*

Preceded by a Genitive, *ը* or *ն* for all the persons of the Plural.

The forms *երնիս*, *երնիդ* and *երնին* are appended to monosyllables ; *նիս*, *նիդ* and *նին* to words of more than one syllable.

The suffix for the 3 p. Sing. and for the Pl. is *ը* when the word to which it is appended terminates with a consonant, and ՛ն when it terminates with a vowel. (՛ also becomes ՛ն before a word commencing with a vowel, provided the two words are pronounced in close connexion.

In signification these suffixes are generally *possessive*, and in conjunction with the Gen. case of nouns or of the Personal or Demonstrative pronouns constitute the usual mode of indicating the idea of possession ; e. g. Իմ տունս *my house*, անոնց վիճակը *their condition.*

Sometimes however they are personal and in apposition with the nouns to which they are appended ; as Վա՛յ ձեզի փարիսեցիներուդ *woe unto you Pharisees!* When appended to prepositions, they are of course personal, as քու վրադ *upon thee*, մէջերնիս *among us.*

The Sing. Suffixes are appended to all the cases of nouns. A noun with a plural suffix is thus declined.

Nom. & Acc. Աչքերնիս *our eyes.*
Gen. & Dat. աչքերնուս
Abl. Աչքերնուս *or* աչքերնէս
Inst. Աչքերովնիս

The plural suffixes when they include the syllable եր (which forms the plural of nouns) are somewhat ambiguous ; thus տուներնիդ may signify *your house* or *your houses.* To express this distinction clearly in Armenian we must say, for the former ձեր տունը , and for the latter ձեր տուները .

In like manner the suffixes ս and դ or ն are used as demonstratives after աս and ան ; as բարև աս տունս *peace to this house*, (Matt. 10 : 12), ան տունէն *from that house* v. 14. This latter however coalesces with the definite form of the noun. So does ը or ն when used as a possessive suffix. They must be distinguished by the connexion. That this suffix has however a possessive force, and is not always to be eckoned as a demonstrative pronoun or a definiter article, is evident from such phrases as *մասնց մէկը* *one of these*, *Թագաւորին մէկը* *a certain king*, *ուրիշ չկայ* *there is no other than he* ; also from the analogy of the possesive suffixes of the other persons.

The separate *Poesessive* pronouns, as has been re-marked above, are the same with the Genitive cases of the personal pronouns, as *իմ* or *իմին* *my*, *մեր* or *մերին* *our*, &c. When the substantive to which they belong is understood and they correspond to *mine, thine*, &c. they are declined like nouns, taking pleonastically their appropriate suffixes ; thus.

	Sing.	Plur.
Nom. & Acc.	իմս or իմինս	իմիններս mine
Gen. & Dat.	իմինիս	իմիններուս of or to mine
Abl. &	իմինէս	իմիններէս from mine
Inst.	իմինովս	իմիններովս

In like manner are declined *քուկդ* or *քուկինդ thine, իրը* or *իրէնը his, hers, its, մերը* or *մերինը ours, ձերը* or *ձերինը yours*, and *իրէնցը theirs*, the oblique cases being always derived from the dissyllabic forms.

VERBS.

The simplest form of he Verb in modern Armenian is the Infinitive Mood, which may therefore be pro-perly regarded as the root, although in most Ancient

Armenian Lexicons the Present Indicative is so regarded.

Verbs have in the Infinitive Mood four terminations, viz. *ալ*, *ել*, *իլ*, and *ուլ*.

MOODS AND TENSES.

The Moods are five ; the Indicative, Imperative, Subjunctive, Potential or Conditional, and Infinitive. Their use does not differ materially from that of the corresponding moods of English verbs, except that the Infinitive is also a Gerund, and as such is declined, both definitely and indefinitely, like nouns. Thus *գործել* to work, working, *գործելու* of or for working, *գործելէ* from working , *գործելը* the working, *գործելուն* of the working, &c.

The Tenses are seven, the Present, Imperfect Aorist, Perfect, Pluperfect, First Future, and Second Future. Respecting their use, see below, p. 47.

FORMATION OF THE TENSES.

The present Tense of the Indicative is formed from the Infinitive by changing its final *լ* into *մ* and prefixng the syllable *կը* (in the case of monosyllabic roots *կու*) ; as *բանալ* to open, *կը բանամ* I open ; *սիրել* to love *կը սիրեմ* I love ; *խօսիլ* to speak *կը խօսիմ* I speak ; *թողուլ* to leave, *կը թողում* I leave ; *լալ* to cry, *կուլամ* I cry.

The Imperfect is formed from the Present by changing its final *ամ* into *այի*, *եմ* or *իմ* into *էի* and *ում* into *ույի* , as *կը բանայի*, *կը սիրէի*, *կը թողույի* , *կու լայի*.

The prefix *կը* appears only in the Present and Imperfect Indicative. The following verbs do not take it even in these tenses ; *եմ* I am, *կրնամ* I can, *գիտեմ* I know and *ունիմ* I have. *կարծեմ* I think, sometimes takes it, and sometimes not. *կը կարծեմ* expresses an opinion with rather more confidence than *կարծեմ* .

The Aorist * varies in different verbs, and must be learned from the Lexicon. Nevertheless the following general principles will be of use to the student.

1. Regular active verbs in *ել* change this termination into *եցի* to form the Aorist, as *կատարել* to finish, Aor. *կատարեցի* .

2. Causative verbs in *ցրնել* or *ցունել* change this termination into *ցուցի* , as *սեւցրնել* to blacken, Aor. *սեւցուցի* •

3. Verbs in *ալ* (except those in *նալ*) agree with those in *ել* , making the Aorist in *ացի* , as *աղալ* , to grind, Aor. *աղացի* .

4. Those in *նալ* generally make the Aor. in *ցայ* , as *մոռնալ* to forget, *մոռցայ* , *ուրանալ* to deny, *ուրացայ* •

5. Verbs in *իլ* (and *նիլ* preceded by a vowel) change this termination into *եցայ* , as *խօսիլ* , *խօսեցայ* • This rule includes all regular Passive verbs.

6. Verbs terminating in *նիլ* preceded by a consonant, form the Aorist by changing this termination into *այ* , as *մեռնիլ* to die, Aor. *մեռայ* ; *հասնիլ* to arrive, Aor. *հասայ* •

The Perfect and Pluperfect are formed by combining the Past Participle of the principal verb with the Present and Imperfect of the auxiliary *եմ* † .

---

*I call this tense *Aorist* (though the Armenian grammarians call it Perfect) because it corresponds in sense with the Greek Aorist, and because the Armenian has another Perfect, corresponding in form and use with the Perfect in other languages.

†More rarely *ունիմ* I have ; as *տեսած ունիմ* I have seen, instead of *տեսած եմ* •

The first or simple Future is formed by prefixing *պիտի* to the Subjunctive Present, which is, in regular verbs, the same as the Indicative Present without the prefix *կը*. Thus *պիտի գործեմ* *I shall work* (lit. *it must be that I work*, or *it is necessary that I work*).

The Future Participle combined with the Present tense of *եմ* gives another form of this tense.

The Second or compound Future consists of the First Future of the auxiliary *եմ* and the Past Participle of the principal verb.

The formation of the tenses in the other moods will be seen in the Paradigms.

THE AUXILIARY VERB *եմ* I am.

The substantive verb *եմ* *I am*, being an auxiliary, first claims attention. It is strictly a defective verb, its wanting tenses being supplied from *ըլլալ* *to become*. It is thus varied.

INDICATIVE MOOD.

PRESENT.

Singular.	*Plural.*
եմ I am	*ենք* we are
ես thou art	*եք* ye are
է he, she, *or* it is	*են* they are

IMPERFECT.

էի I was	*էինք* we were
էիր thou wast	*էիք* ye were
էր he was	*էին* they were

AORIST.

Եղայ I was   Եղանք we were
Եղար thou wast Եղաք ye were
Եղաւ he was   Եղան they were

PERFECT.

Եղած եմ I have been Եղած ենք we have been
Եղած ես thou hast been Եղած էք ye have been
Եղած է he has been Եղած են they have been
 or Եղեր եմ, Եղեր ես, &c.

PLUPERFECT.

Եղած էի I had been   Եղած էինք we had been
Եղած էիր thou hadst been Եղած էիք ye had been
Եղած էր he had been   Եղած էին they had been
 or Եղեր էի, Եղեր էիր, &c.

FIRST FUTURE.

Պիտի ըլլամ I shall be Պիտի ըլլանք we shall be
Պիտի ըլլաս thou wilt be Պիտի ըլլաք ye will be
Պիտի ըլլայ he will be   Պիտի ըլլան they will be
 or Ըլլալու եմ, Ըլլալու ես, Ըլլալու է, &c.

SECOND FUTURE.

Պիտի եղած ըլլամ, or եղած պիտի ըլլամ, ըլլաս, &c.
I shall have been

IMPERATIVE MOOD.

Թող ըլլամ let me be   Թող ըլլանք let us be
Եղիր be thou   Եղէք or եղիք be ye
Թող ըլլայ let him be   Թող ըլլան let them be

SUBJUNCTIVE MOOD.

PRESENT AND FIRST FUTURE.

Ւլլամ that *or* if I be   Ւլանք that *or* if we be
Ւլաս that *or* if thou be   Ւլաք that *or* if ye be
Ւլայ that *or* if he be   Ւլան that *or* if they be

IMPERFECT.

Ւլայի that *or* if I were   Ւլայիևք that *or* if we were
Ւլայիր that *or* if thou   Ւլայիք that *or* if ye were
    wert
Ւլար that *or* if he were   Ւլայիև that *or* if they
                               were

PERFECT AND SECOND FUTURE.

Եղած ըլլամ , ըլլաս , &c. that *or* if I have been, *or*
shall have been

PLUPERFECT.

Եղած ըլլայի · ըլլայիր , &c. that *or* if I should have
been

FUTURE

[beside the form of the Present].

Ւլալու ըլլամ , ըլլաս , &c. that *or* if I should hereafter
be

POTENTIAL *or* CONDITIONAL MOOD.

IMPERFECT.

Պիտի ըլլայի · ըլլայիր , &c. I should be *or* have been

PLUPERFECT.

Պիտի եղած ըլլայի · ըլլայիր , &c. I should have been

INFINITIVE MOOD.

Ըլլալ to be.   Varied as a Gerund, ըլլալու of being, ըլլալէ from being, ըլլալով with, by, *or* on account of being.

PARTICIPLES.

Present Եղող [*or* ըլլող] being
Past Եղած *or* եղեր having been.
Future Ըլլալու about to be.

———

Of the four endings of Regular Verbs եմ is the most frequent. An example in that ending will therefore be given in full.

CONJUGATION of the REGULAR VERB ԳՈՐԾԵՄ to work.

ACTIVE VOICE.

INDICATIVE MOOD.

PRESENT.

I work *or* I am working

Singular.	Plural.
Կը գործեմ	Կը գործենք*
Կը գործես	Կը գործէք
Կը գործէ	Կը գործեն

IMPERFECT.

I was working *or* I wrought habitually

Կը գործէի	Կը գործէինք
Կը գործէիր	Կը գործէիք
Կը գործէր	Կը գործէին

———

* Some use ենք as the termination of the 1st pers. Plur. conforming to the Ancient Armenian. But this is considered pedantic.

AORIST.

I wrought or I have wrought

Գործեցի　　　　　　　　Գործեցինք

Գործեցիր　　　　　　　Գործեցիք

Գործեց　　　　　　　　Գործեցին

PERFECT.

I have wrought

Գործած եմ　　　　　　Գործած ենք

Գործած ես　　　　　　Գործած էք

Գործած է　　　　　　　Գործած են

or Գործեր եմ, գործեր ես, &c.

PLUPERFECT.

I had wrought

Գործած էի　　　　　　Գործած էինք

Գործած էիր　　　　　　Գործած էիք

Գործած էր　　　　　　Գործած էին

or Գործեր էի, գործեր էիր, &c.

FIRST FUTURE.

I shall work or I will work

Պիտի գործեմ　　　　　Պիտի գործենք

Պիտի գործես　　　　　Պիտի գործէք

Պիտի գործէ　　　　　Պիտի գործեն

or Գործելու եմ, գործելու ես, &c.

SECOND FUTURE.

I shall have wrought

Գործած պիտի ըլլամ　　　　Գործած պիտի ըլլանք

Գործած պիտի ըլլաս　　　　Գործած պիտի ըլլաք

Գործած պիտի ըլլայ　　　　Գործած պիտի ըլլան

or Պիտի գործած ըլլամ, &.

IMPERATIVE MOOD.

Թող գործեմ let me work   Թող գործենք let us work
Գործէ́ work thou   Գործեցէք work ye
Թող գործէ let him work   Թող գործեն let them work

SUBJUNCTIVE MOOD.

PRESENT AND FIRST FUTURE.

That I work *or* if I work

Գործեմ   Գործենք
Գործես   Գործէք
Գործէ   Գործեն

IMPERFECT.

That *or* if I should work

Գործէի   Գործէինք
Գործէիր   Գործէիք
Գործէր   Գործէին

PERFECT AND SECOND FUTURE.

That *or* if I have wrought, *or* should have wrought

Գործած ըլլամ   Գործած ըլլանք
Գործած ըլլաս   Գործած ըլլաք
Գործած ըլլայ   Գործած ըլլան

PLUPERFECT.

That *or* if I had wrought, *or* should have wrought

Գործած ըլլայի   Գործած ըլլայինք
Գործած ըլլայիր   Գործած ըլլայիք
Գործած ըլլար   Գործած ըլլային

FIRST FUTURE.

[2d form] That *or* if I should hereafter work

Գործելու ըլլամ   Գործելու ըլլանք
Գործելու ըլլաս   Գործելու ըլլաք
Գործելու ըլլայ   Գործելու ըլլան

POTENTIAL or CONDITIONAL MOOD.

IMPERFECT.

I would *or* should work *or* have wrought

Պիտի գործէի   Պիտի գործէինք

Պիտի գործէիր   Պիտի գործէիք

Պիտի գործէր   Պիտի գործէին

PLUPERFECT.

I would *or* should have wrought

Պիտի գործած ըլլայի   Պիտի գործած ըլլայինք

Պիտի գործած ըլլայիր   Պիտի գործած ըլլայիք

Պիտի գործած ըլլար   Պիտի գործած ըլլային

INFINITIVE MOOD.

PRESENT.

Գործել to work. Varied as a Gerund thus; Gen. and Dat. գործելու, Abl. գործելէ. Inst գործելով, of, to, from, by, working.

PERFECT.

Գործած ըլլալ to have wrought. Varied in like manner, Gen. and Dat. գործած ըլլալու, Abl. գործած ըլլալէ, Inst. գործած ըլլալով, of, to, from, by, having wrought.

PARTICIPLES.

PRESENT.

Գործող [or գործօղ] working.

PAST.

Գործեր or գործած having wrought.

FUTURE.

Գործելու about to work.

PASSIVE VOICE.
INDICATIVE MOOD.

PRESENT.

Կը գործուիմ *　　　　　Կը գործուինք
Կը գործուիս　　　　　　Կը գործուիք
Կը գործուի　　　　　　　Կը գործուին

IMPERFECT.

Կը գործուէի　　　　　　Կը գործուէինք
Կը գործուէիր　　　　　　Կը գործուէիք
Կը գործուէր　　　　　　Կը գործուէին

AORIST.

Գործուեցայ　　　　　　Գործուեցանք
Գործուեցար　　　　　　Գործուեցաք
Գործուեցաւ　　　　　　Գործուեցան

PERFECT.

Գործուած եմ　　　　　Գործուած ենք
Գործուած ես　　　　　　Գործուած էք
Գործուած է　　　　　　Գործուած են
　　or Գործուեր եմ

PLUPERFECT.

Գործուած էի　　　　　Գործուած էինք
Գործուած էիր　　　　　Գործուած էիք
Գործուած էր　　　　　Գործուած էին
　　or Գործուեր էի

FIRST FUTURE.

Պիտի գործուիմ　　　　Պիտի գործուինք
Պիտի գործուիս　　　　Պիտի գործուիք
Պիտի գործուի　　　　　Պիտի գործուին
　　or Գործուելու եմ

*Also written կը գործըուիմ, կը գործըուիս, &c.

6

SECOND FUTURE.

Պիտի գործուած ըլլամ   Պիտի գործուած ըլլանք
Պիտի գործուած ըլլաս   Պիտի գործուած ըլլաք
Պիտի գործուած ըլլայ   Պիտի գործուած ըլլան

IMPERATIVE MOOD.

Թող գործուիմ   Թող գործուինք
Գործուէ   Գործուցէք
Թող գործուի   Թող գործուին

SUBJUNCTIVE MOOD.

PRESENT AND FIRST FUTURE.

Գործուիմ   Գործուինք
Գործուիս   Գործուիք
Գործուի   Գործուին

IMPERFECT.

Գործուէի   Գործուէինք
Գործուէիր   Գործուէիք
Գործուէր   Գործուէին

PERFECT AND SECOND FUTURE.

Գործուած ըլլամ   Գործուած ըլլանք
Գործուած ըլլաս   Գործուած ըլլաք
Գործուած ըլլայ   Գործուած ըլլան

PLUPERFECT.

Գործուած ըլլայի   Գործուած ըլլայինք
Գործուած ըլլայիր   Գործուած ըլլայիք
Գործուած ըլլար   Գործուած ըլլային

FIRST FUTURE.

Գործուելու ըլլամ   Գործուելու ըլլանք
Գործուելու ըլլաս   Գործուելու ըլլաք
Գործուելու ըլլայ   Գործուելու ըլլան

POTENTIAL or CONDITIONAL MOOD.

IMPERFECT.

Պիտի գործուէի

PLUPERFECT.

Պիտի գործուած ըլլայի

INFINITIVE MOOD.

PRESENT.

Գործուիլ , գործուելու &c.

PERFECT.

Գործուած ըլլալ , ըլլալու , &c.

PARTICIPLES.

PRESENT. Գործուող

PAST. Գործուած or գործուեր

FUTURE. Գործուելու

———

OF VERBS TERMINATING IN ել, իլ, and ուլ.

Verbs in ալ preserve the ա throughout the Indicative, Imperative, Subjunctive, Potential and Infinitive Active ; as կարդալ to read, Pres. Ind. կը կարդամ, կը կարդաս, կը կարդայ. կը կարդանք, կը կարդաք, կը կարդան . Imp. կը կարդայի , կը կարդայիր , կը կարդաք, &c. Aor. կարդացի &c. The present and Past Participles generally take an additional syllable derived from the form of the Aorist ; as կարդացող , կարդացեր , կարդացած . The last two appear of course in the compound tenses of the Verb. The Passive Voice also exhibits this additional syllable ; as կը կարդացուի it is read.

Verbs in *նալ* generally make the Aorist Indicative in *ցայ* and the Imperative in *ցիր*, as *մոռնամ to forget*, *մոռցայ*, *մոռցիր*. But *բանամ* makes *բացի* and *բաց*.

Those in *իլ* are generally declined like the Passive voice; as *կը խօսիմ I speak*, *կը խօսիս*, *կը խօսի*, &c. Imp. *կը խօսէի*, Aor. *խօսեցայ*. Imperative *խօսէ*, Participles *խօսող*, *խօսեր*, *խօսած*. But some, especially those which terminate in *նիմ* preceded by a consonant change that termination into *այ* for the Aorist and into *իր* for the Imperative; as *մեռնիլ to die*, Aor. *մեռայ*, Imp. *մեռիր*.

I believe the only verb in *ուլ* now in use is *թողուլ to leave* or *permit*, which preserves its proper wovel and like verbs in *ամ* has the additional syllable in the Present and Past Participles; thus *կը թողում*, *կը թողուս*, *կը թողու*. *կը թողունք*, *կը թողուք*, *կը թողուն* : Imp. *կը թողուի*, Aor. *թողուցի*, Participles *թողուցող*, *թողուցեր*, *թողուցած*.

COMPARATIVE VIEW OF THE DIFFERENT CLASSES OF REGULAR VERBS.

In order to aid the learner in becoming familiar with the forms of these different classes of verbs, a table is subjoined exhibiting several examples of each kind with their principal forms.

TABLE OF THE PRINCIPAL FORMS OF VERBS.

Infinitive	Aor. Ind.	Imperative	Pres. Part.	Past Part.

Verbs terminating in ել.

Infinitive	Aor. Ind.	Imperative	Pres. Part.	Past Part.
Գործել to work	գործեցի	գործէ՛	գործող	գործած or գործեր
Կանչել to call	կանչեցի	կանչէ՛	կանչող	կանչած or կանչեր
Կնքել to seal	կնքեցի	կնքէ՛	կնքող	կնքած or կնքեր
Համբերել to be patient	համբերեցի	համբերէ՛	համբերող	համբերած or համբերեր

Causative verbs ending in ցնել.

Infinitive	Aor. Ind.	Imperative	Pres. Part.	Past Part.
Աւելցնել to add	աւելցուցի	աւելցո՛ւ	աւելցնող	աւելցուցած or աւելցուցեր
Խենթեցնել to craze	խենթեցուցի	խենթեցո՛ւ	խենթեցնող	խենթեցուցած or խենթեցուցեր
Մոռցնել to cause to forget	մոռցուցի	մոռցո՛ւ	մոռցնող	մոռցուցած or մոռցուցեր
Սեւցնել to blacken	սեւցուցի	սեւցո՛ւ	սեւցնող	սեւցուցած or սեւցուցեր

Verbs in ալ generally.

Infinitive	Aor. Ind.	Imperative	Pres. Part.	Past Part.
Աղալ to grind	աղացի	աղա՛	աղացող	աղացած or աղացեր
Զգալ to feel	զգացի	զգա՛	զգացող	զգացած or զգացեր
Լալ to cry	լացի	լա՛	լացող	լացած or լացեր
Խնդալ to laugh	խնդացի	խնդա՛	խնդացող	խնդացած or խնդացեր

Infinitive	Aor. Ind.	Imperative.	Pres. Part.	Past Part.

Verbs in _ .

Infinitive	Aor. Ind.	Imperative.	Pres. Part.	Past Part.
to turn				
to wonder				
to mount				
to deny				

Verbs in _ (and _ preceded by a vowel).

Infinitive	Aor. Ind.	Imperative.	Pres. Part.	Past Part.
to toil				
to trust				
to confess				
to quit				

Verbs terminating in _ preceded by a consonant.

Infinitive	Aor. Ind.	Imperative.	Pres. Part.	Past Part.
to pass				
to arrive				
to be exhausted				
to die				

Verbs in ____.

to fly			
Թռչիլ or Թռիլ tr fly			
Կորնչիլ to be lost (See also կորսուիլ below.)			
Անդչիլ to repose			
Մարտնչիլ to fight			
Փախչիլ OR փախիլ to flee			

Verb in ____.

Թողուլ to leave

Passive verbs.

Գործուիլ to be wrought
Գրուիլ to be written
Խրկուիլ to be sent
Կորսուիլ to be lost
Պահուիլ to be kept

ETYMOLOGY.

NEGATIVE VERBS.

The negative of the auxiliary *եմ* is formed by prefixing the letter *չ* ; as *չեմ* I am not, *չէ* he, she, or *it is not*. The same rule applies to *կայ* there is, and to *ունիմ* I have ; as *չկար* there was not, *չունէիք* we have not, Also substantially to all the tenses of the regular Verb* except the Present and Imperfect Indicative. The Negative form of these two tenses is obtained by prefixing the Negative of the auxilary verb for these two tenses to a participial form ending in *ր* and derived from the root by changing its final *լ* into that letter, as *չեմ բանար* I do not open, *չեմ թողուր* I do not leave. If the verb terminate in *ել*, this participle, though Present in signification, coincides in form with the Past Participle in *եր*, as *չեմ գործեր* ; if in *ալ*, *իլ*, or *ուլ*, it does not ; as *չեմ յուսար*, Past Participle *յուսացեր*, *չեմ տանիր*, Past Participle *տարեր*, *չեմ թողուր*, Past Participle, *թողուցեր* :

In the 3d pers. Sing. of the Present tense the Auxiliary is dropped, and the Participle only appears with the negative prefix.

Some writers instead of uniformly employing a simple *չ* use *չի* (as a separate word) when the verb begins with a consonat and *չ* (as a prefix) only when it begins with a wowel ; thus, *չի կայ* there is not, *չի տեսայ* I did not see. But *չկայ* and *չտեսայ* appear to be in accordance with the most approved usage.

In tenses formed by a participle and an auxiliary the negative prefix is attached to the auxiliary and not to the participle. In the Future it may be attached either to *պիտի* or to the verb. The latter is most approved.

It will be sufficient to give the forms of the negative verb for the Indicative Mood ; thus

*For the negative form of the Imperative see below.

PRESENT TENSE.

Sing.

Չեմ գործեր ,   I am not working,
Չես գործեր ,   thou art not working,
Չգործեր .   he is not working ;

Plur.

Չենք գործեր ,   we are not working,
Չէք գործեր ,   ye are not working,
Չեն գործեր :   they are not working.

Imp. չէի գործեր , չէիր գործեր , չէր գործեր , &c.
Aor. չգործեցի , չգործեցիր , չգործեց , &c.
Perf. գործած չեմ , գործած չես , գործած չէ , &c.
Plup. գործած չէի , գործած չէիր , &c.
First Fut. պիտի չգործեմ , պիտի չգործես , պիտի չգոր֊
ծէ , &c. or չպիտի գործեմ , &c.
Second Fut. գործած պիտի չըլլամ or գործած չպիտի
ըլլամ .

The negative particle for the 2d person of the
Imperative is not չ but մի̈ . (Compare the Greek μή).
The form of the verb in that person is derived from
the Infinitive by changing its final լ into ր for the Singular and into ք for the Plural.

The paradigm of the Imperative negative verb will
therefore stand thus ;

Sing.

1 Թող չգործեմ ,   let me not work,
2 Մի̈ գործեր ,   do not (thou) work,
3 Թող չգործէ .   let him not work ;

Plur.

1 Թող չգործենք ,   let us not work,
2 Մի̈ գործէք ,   do not (ye) work,
3 Թող չգործեն :   let them not work.

7

IMPERSONAL VERBS.

These are regularly conjugated so far as the third person singular is concerned ; thus *կ՚անձրեւէ* *it rains,* Imperfect *կ՚անձրեւէր* *it was raining,* Aorist *անձրեւեց* *it rained* or *has rained,* First Future *պիտի անձրեւէ* *it will rain,* &c.

կայ *there is* is used only in the Present and Imperfect tenses of the Indicative Mood. Unlike other impersonal verbs, it has a plural form, as follows.
Present Sing. *կայ* there is   Plur. *կան* there are.
Imperfect Sing. *կար* there was, Plur. *կային* there were

Intransitive verbs sometimes exhibit a Passive form, used impersonally, and denoting the *possibility* of performing the action expressed by those verbs ; thus *կ՚ելլուի* *it is possible to go up,* from *ելլել* *to go up,* *կ՚երթուի* or *կ՚երդւագուի* *it is possible to go,* from *երթալ* *to go.* (Comp. the Latin *curritur.*) They are used for the most part with a negative ; as *չերթւագուիր* *it is impossible to go.*

DERIVATIVE VERBS.

By adding *նալ* or *անալ* to almost any adjective a verb may be formed, signifying to acquire the quality expressed by the adjective ; e. g. from *բարձր* *high* comes *բարձրանալ* *to be elevated,* from *աղքատ* *poor* comes *աղքատանալ* *to become poor,* &c.

Verbs ending in *ցընել* or *գուցնել* are *Causative,* and are derived, generally from Neuter, but in a few instances from active verbs by changing the termination of the Aorist, *ցի*, *ցայ*, or *այ* when that tense has not *ց* in its last syllable, into *ցընել* ; as *կարդալ* *to read*, Aor. *կարդացի*, Causative verb *կարդացընել* to *cause to read*, to *instruct in reading* ; *մոռնալ* to *forget*, Aor. *մոռցայ*. Caus. v. *մոռցընել* to *cause to forget* ; *հասնիլ* to *arrive*, Aor. *հասայ*, Caus. v. *հասցընել* to *cause to arrive* ; *ուտել* to *eat*, Aor. irreg. *կերայ*, Caus. v. *կերցընել* to *cause to eat*, to *feed*.

Those verbs which do not form Causatives, supply their place by the various forms of *տալ* to *give*, here in the sense of *to cause*, with their own Infinitive ; e. g. *գործել տալ* to *cause to work*, to *set at work* , *գործեցընել* not being authorized by good usage. So *ելլել* to *rise*, though a neuter verb has no Causative, and consequently we must say *ելլել տալ* ; or the place of this phrase may be supplied by some other verb, as *վերցընել* or *հանել* • We may also say *վերցընիլ տալ* , *մեռցընել տալ* to *employ another to raise, to kill*, &c.

IRREGULAR VERBS.

These are not numerous, and their anomalies are chiefly confined to the Aorist Indicative, the Imperative and the Participles. The Present Imperfect and Future of the Indicative, and the simple tenses of the Subjunctive, are uniformly regular. The compound tenses, of course, follow the Participles.

Those Aorists which end in *այ* are declined like the Aorist of Passive verbs. Thus *եկայ* , *եկար* , *եկաւ* , *եկանք* , *եկաք* *եկան* . Those ending in *ի* also take *աւ* in the third person singular ; as *առի* , *առիր* , *առաւ* , *առինք* , *առիք* , *առին* • But *գացի* becomes in the third person Sing. *գնաց* •

LIST OF IRREGULAR VERBS WITH THEIR PRINCIPAL PARTS.

Infinitive.	Aor.	Imper.	Pres. Part.	Past Part.
Առնել to take	առի	ա՛ռ	առնող	առած or առեր
Գալ to come	եկայ	եկ՛ or եկող or եկած or եկեր եկո՛ւր		գալող
Գիտնել or գիտ-նալ to know	գիտցայ	գիտցիր	գիտցող	գիտցած or գիտ-ցեր
Գտնել to find	գտայ	գտիր	գտնող	գտած or գտեր
Դնել to put	դրի	դիր	դնող	դրած or դրեր
Ելլել or ելլալ to rise	ելայ	ելիր or ելլող ել		ելած or ելեր
For Եմ see ըլլալ.				
Երթալ to go	գացի or գնաց	գնա՛	{ գացող գնացող or երթող	գացած or գացեր }
Զարնել to strike	զարկի	զա՛րկ	զարնող	զարկած or զար-կեր
Ըլլալ to be	եղայ	եղիր	եղող or ըլլող	եղած or եղեր
Ընել to do	ըրի	ըրէ	ընող	ըրած or ըրեր
Ըսել to say	ըսի	ըսէ	ըսող	ըսած or ըսեր
Թքնել to spit	թքի or թու՛ք թուքի	թքնող	թքած, թուքած, թքեր or թուքեր	
Իյնալ to fall	{ ինկայ ընկայ	ինկիր ընկիր	ինկող իյնող	ինկած, ինկեր, ընկած or ընկեր }
Իջնել to des-cend	իջայ	իջիր	իջնող	իջած, or իջեր
Մտնել to enter	մտայ	մտիր	մտնող	մտած or մտեր
Ուտել to eat	կերայ	կե՛ր	ուտող	կերած or կերեր
Տալ to give	տուի	տո՛ւր	տուող	տուած or տուեր
Տանիլ to carry	տարի	տա՛ր	տանող	տարած or տարեր
Տեսնել to see	տեսայ	տե՛ս or տեսնող տեսի՛ր		տեսած or տեսեր

The Passive of դնել is դրուիլ , of տալ , տրուիլ ·
(or տացուիլ) and of տանիլ , տարուիլ . Ընել has no
proper passive, but ըլլալ is employed instead in the
sense of *to be done*.

USE OF THE TENSES.

The Present ordinarily desigates either present or
habitual action ; as կը գրեմ *I am writing* , or simply *I
write*. It is not unfrequently however used as a Future,
especially in giving a promise ; as կ'երթամ *I will go* ;
also as a Potential ; as կը կարդացուի *it can be read, it
is legible,* կ'ըլլայ *it can be done.*

The Imperfect expresses

(a) Action past, but incomplete at the time referred
to ; as կը կարդար *he was reading* ;

(b) Repeated action ; as կը քարոզէր *he was in the
habit of preaching* ;

(c) Conditional action ; as կու տայի թէ որ . . . *I
would give,* or *I would have given, if* . . .

The *Aorist* or *Simple Preterite* is the historic tense.
It states an action as completed in past time, specified
or not, and having or not having a relation to the
Present ; as գրեցի *I wrote,* or *I have written.*

The *Perfect* or *Compound Preterite* seems to express
primarily the idea of *being in the position of one who did
or has done any thing.* Thus գրած եմ or գրեր եմ , (lit.
I am having written) *I occupy the position of one who wrote
or has written.* That this tense has not always the
same reference to the present time which our English Perfect has, is evident from the fact that it is
used with specifications of Past time, when the state
of things implied by the recorded action continues ,
thus երկուշաբթիեն գեղը գացեր է , *As long ago a's*

Monday he went to the country (and remains there still).

Hence the Aorist and Perfect may often be used indifferently ; as 'Ն ամակները գրեցիր, or գրա՞ծ ես , *Have you written the letters ?* գրեցի, or գրած եմ , *I have written them* ; the former referring simply to the action performed, the latter alluding to the condition of the actor after having accomplished his task.

This secondary or indirect mode of bringing out the idea of a past action gives rise to another use of their Perfect, viz. to state a fact, of which the the narrator has not been an eye-witness, or which he has learned from circumstantial evidence. Thus if I say Յովհաննէս գրեր է այս նամակը , it means *I have been informed* or *I have reason believe that John wrote this letter* ; but if I say . . . գրեց . . . then every Armenian will understand me as affirming that I saw him write it, or at least that I know the fact in the most positive manner. See also the remark on եղեր , p. 51.

Of the two participial forms from which this tense is compounded, the one in ած possesses more of an adjective character than that in եր ; (hence the use of such phrases as իմ ծախած տունս *the house which I sold*, the form in եր not being employed in a similar way ;) and to this we may perhaps attribute the fact that the Perfect with a negative employs exclusively the form in ած ; as գրած չեմ ; *I have not written.* We cannot say գրեր չեմ , and չեմ գրեր is Present ; though colloquially the չ of the negative Perfect is sometimes prefixed to the participial form, and then either ending may be used indifferently ; thus չգրած եմ , or չգրեր եմ , *I have not written.*

OF CERTAIN PARTICLES OCCASIONALLY APPENDED
TO VERBS.

The syllable *կոր* is colloquially added to the several persons of the Present and Imperfect tenses of verbs to give emphasis ; as *կը բանամ կոր* *I am actually now opening,* *կը գործես կոր* *thou art actually working,* &c.

The syllable *նէ* is frequently added to verbs in the Subjunctive Mood ; as *Ո'վ որ գործէ նէ* *whoever work ;* also to the Indicative, giving it the force of a Subjunctive ; as *Ուր որ կերթաս նէ* *wherever you go ;* sometimes it has the sense of *թէ որ* *if,* and in that case *թէ որ* may be omitted ; as *Որ որ ըսես նէ* or simply *ըսես նէ* *If you say.*

Եղեր , the Past Participle of the Verb *ըլլալ* *to be,* (like the Turkish *imish*) appended to a verb in the Present or a past tense, implies that the fact stated is not one of which the narrator has been an eyewitness, but that he has been informed of it by some one else, and is nearly equivalent to *I am informed,* or *It must be that* ; Thus *Կհասկնամ որ կու գայ եղեր* *I understand that the King is coming.*

Մի appended to verbs is interrogative ; as *կու գաս մի* *are you coming ?*

All these particles belong to the language of conversation, rather than to that of books. Indeed the best writers now entirely avoid them.

ADVERBS.

Adverbs are either

1 Primitive ; as *հիմա* *now,* *երէկ* *yesterday,* *վաղը* *to-*

morrow, *մշտ* *always*, *հոս* *here*, *հոն* *there*, *այո* *yes*, *ոչ* , *չէ* , *no*, &c. or

2 Derived from other parts of speech ; e. g.

(a) Adjectives without change ; as *շատ* *much*, *քիչ* *little*, *սուտ* *falsely*, *անողորմ* *unmercifully*, *անյոյս* *hopelessly*, &c.

(b) Adjectives with the termination *պէս* or *բար* joined by a union-vowel, generally *ա* ; as *հոգեւորապէս* *spiritually*, from *հոգեւոր* *spiritual*, *յիմարաբար* *foolishly*, form *յիմար* *foolish*. Adjectives having *է* in their last syllable change it into *ի* in the Adverbs derived from them ; and those having *ի* or *ու* drop them ; as *տգէտ* *ignorant*, *տգիտաբար* *ignorantly*, *սաստիկ* *vehement*, *սաստ_ կապէս* *vehemently*, *ծածուկ* *secret*, *ծածկաբար* *secretly*. Compare the changes occurring in the declension of nouns. See p. 18.

(c) Nouns in the Instrumental case ; as *գիշերով* *by night*, *ցորեկով* *by day* ; *սրտով* *heartily*, *անիրաւու_ թեամբ* *unjustly*, *տգիտութեամբ* *ignorantly*. Sometimes the form of the Ancient Armenian Instrumental is preserved ; as *կարգաւ* *in an orderly manner*, *կարծեօք* *by conjecture*.

(d) Nouns in the Ablative case ; as *շատոնցմէ* or *շատոնցուընէ* *of a long time*, *a long time ago*, *առտուընէ* *ever since morning*, or with a form derived from the Anc. Arm. Abl. Plur. *առտուանց* *in the morning*, *գիշե_ րուանց* *by night*.

(e) Nouns resembling the form of the Genitive, but, by an ellipsis of *'ի in*, having the force of the ancient Commorative or Locative case ; as *մութուն* *in the dark*, *ցորեկին* *in the day time*, *մութնուլուսուն* *at dawn*, *կէս գիշերին* *at midnight*.

(f) Nouns repeated ; as *տուն տուն* *from house to house*, *քաղաք քաղաք* *from city to city.*

(g) The names of languages terminating in *րէն* and derived from gentile nouns ; as *Հայերէն* in *Armenian,* *Յունարէն* in *Greek,* *Անգղիարէն* in *English* &c. Somewhat resembling these are also *մարդկորէն* *humanly,* *ռամկորէն* *vulgarly,* &c. although these are perhaps from *օրէն* in the sense of *custom, manner.*

(h) Adjectives or adjective pronouns and nouns combined ; as *զուր տեղը* *in vain,* *այն ատեն* *then.*

(i) Infinitives (as Gerunds) in the Instrumental case, with or without the negative prefix ; as *չգիտնալով* *ignorantly,* *չմտածելով* *thoughtlessly,* *ուրախութեամբ* *with pleasure.*

Adverbs admit a diminutive termination as well as Adjectives ; as *կանուխիկեկ* *rather early,* *ուշիկեկ* *rather late.*

They are sometimes repeated, especially those which have not more than two syllables, to express emphasis ; as *շուտ շուտ* *very quickly,* *ուշ ուշ* *very late.*

PREPOSITIONS.

With the exception of a few retained from the Anc. Arm. (as *ըստ* *according to,* *առանց* *without*) they should rather be called Postpositions, since they uniformly follow the nouns or pronouns which they govern.

Համար *on account of,* requires the Dative, as *ինծի Համար* *for my sake,* or *on account of me.*

Մօտիկ *near,* and *մինչե* *until,* the Dative.

Հետ *with,* the Genitive or Dative.

Ետքէ *after, behind,* the Genitive, or Ablative.

Եռքբ *after* (in time), the Ablative. So also հեռու *far from*, զատ or 'ի զատ *besides*, զազողուկ *without the knowledge of*, (clam).

Most others take the Genitive ; as առջեւ *before*, տեղ *instead of*, առանց *without*, դիմաց *opposite*, տակ *under*, վրայ *upon*, դեմ *over against*, մէջ *in, within*, ձեռոք *by means of*, պէս *like*, քով *near*, ըստ *according to*.

CONJUNCTIONS.

Copulative, եւ , ու *and*, նաեւ *also*, ալ *too*.

Disjunctive, կամ , թէ *either, or*, կամ—եւ կամ , թէ—եւ թէ , *either—or*.

Conditioal, թէ որ , եթէ *if*, եւ (after verbs) *if, although*.

Concessive, թէ եւ , թէպետ , թէպետ եւ *although*, ոչ միայն *not only*.

Adversative, բայց , այլ , հապա , սակայն , *but, yet*, այլ եւ *but also*, այսու ամենայնիւ *nevertheless*.

Diminutive, գոնէ , *at least*.

Causal, ինչու որ , քանզի , վասն զի , *because*, որ *that, because*, որովհետեւ *whereas*.

Rational, ուրեմն *therefore*.

Final, որ *that*, որպէս զի *in order that*.

INTERJECTIONS.

Of calling, ով , ա , այ , հա , O! ձո (addressing a male), քա (addressing a female) *ho! hallo!*

Of encouraging, աղէ , ծն *come on! go to!*

Of praise, վայ , է , ա *how fine!*

Of pity, վախ , էյ (frequently repeated thrice), ախ , ափսոս *alas! wo!* մէ՛զք *what a pity!* վախ or վայհ վայհ *ah!*

Of grief, ախ . վախ , *how sorry I am!*

Of desire, երնէկ , երանէ , երանի թէ , ըլլայ թէ , ուր է որ , ուր եր որ *oh that! would that!*

PART. III.

SYNTAX.

The following peculiarities of construction in Modern Armenian deserve notice.

1. Adjectives uniformly precede the Substantives which they qualify ; as ամէն բան *every thing*. The only exception to this rule is presented by a very few phrases borrowed from the Ancient Armenian ; as Հոգին Սուրբ *the Holy Spirit.*

2. Numerals implying plurality are usually construed with Nouns in the singular ; as չորս մարդ *four men*, իրեք հոգի *three persons*. When the Plural form is employed, it is more emphatic, and sometimes implies that the persons or things spoken of are viewed separately and individually. Thus իրեք օր means *the space of three days* ; իրեք օրերը may be used to signify *the three several days*, or *the several periods of three days each*.

3. In like manner when no numeral is employed, but when other words, as a pronoun or a verb, imply plurality, the noun is usually put in the singular ; as դուք ամէնքդ եղբայր էք *all ye are brethren*, թագաւորին մէկը *a certain king* (i. e. *one of the kings*), մարդուն մէկը *a certain man*.

4. A verb having a Plural nominative is often put in the Singular ; as աչքերս կը գոցուի *my eyes keep shut-*

ling, բերնին շողիքներր վազեց *the saliva ran from his mouth.*
The same is frequently the case when several nouns
in the singular form the subject of the verb ; as գլուխս՝
սիրտս՝ կուրծքս կ՚ցաւի *my head, stomach and breast ache.*

5. The Past Participle of Active verbs, terminating
in ած, is construed with a Genitive of the noun or pronoun designating the *agent,* and with another noun
designating the *object* of a Past action referred to ; as
իմ շինած տունս *the house which I built* or *have built,*
անոնց կարդացած գիրքերը *the books which they read* or
have read.

6. The same Participle of Passive or Neuter verbs
is construed in a similar way, the noun then designating time or place ; as հոն եղած օրս *the day when I was
there,* ժամացոյցին գտնուած տեղը *the place where the watch
was found.*

7. A noun or pronoun in the Accusative, governed
by an active verb, may be placed either before or after
the verb, but more usually precedes it ; as զիս կը սիրէ
(or կը սիրէ զիս) *he loves me* ; իր գործը կատարեց (or կատարեց իր գործը) *he completed his work.*

8. There is a class of active verbs compounded of
a noun and a verb, which though written separately,
constitute only a kind of compound verb, and require
an Accusative ; as պանգ կ՚ընէ իր գործը *he neglects his work,*
համարդ բերան սորվեցա՞ր *have you learned your lesson by
heart ?*

9. For the cases of Nouns and Pronouns required by
Prepositions, see p. 53. The reason why they so frequently govern the Genitive appears to be that they
are (as in Hebrew) radically Substantives. Thus մէջ
in may be regarded as a noun, *the midst,* and therefore
as naturally requiring a Genitive ; as տանը մէջ *the*

midst of the house, in the house. In like manner *աոջևը that which is before,* *տակը that which is under,* *քովը the side,* hence *what is at the side, near,* &c.—This view accounts also for the fact that they sometimes appear in a plural form, as *մէջերը* , *տակերը* , *քովերը* , signifying *somewhere in, somewhere under,* &c. Thus *սեղանին տակերը նայէ look around under the table.*

10. A simple Accusative is often used (by ellipsis of the Anc. Arm. *՛ի*) where we employ *in, at, to,* or *into* ; as *իմ Հայրս որ երկինքն է my Father who is in heaven,* *Պօլիս կը նստին they reside at Constantinople,* *տուն եկաւ he came into a house,* *գիւղը կ'երթամ I am going to the village.*

11. An Ablative without a preposition sometimes signifies *after* ; as *իրեք օրէն after three days,* i. q. *իրեք օրէն ետքը .*

PART IV.

MISCELLANEOUS REMARKS AND IDIOMATIC PHRASES.

1. Respecting the order of words in a sentence some remarks have already been made. See. pp. 49, 51 & 52. It may be remarked in general that the Mod. Arm. in this respect agrees nearly with the Turkish, and varies widely from the European languages and from the Ancient Armenian. Usually, in complex sentences, the circumstances of place and time are first introduced ; then comes the subject, preceded by its adjective if it have one ; then the object of action ; then frequently the circumstances of manner or instrument (although these admit of considerable latitude iu their collocation), and last of all the verb ; thus *Այսօր քաղաքէս փողոցներուն մէկուն մէջ՛ իրեք շոգի իրարու դէմ Հրացաններ*

9

կր պարպէին, To day three persons were firing pistols at each other in one of the streets of this city. *Սինա լեռը Իսրայէլի որդւոց համար Տէրոջը Մովսէսին պատուիրած պատուիրանքները աստէք են*, These are the commandments which the Lord commanded Moses for the children of Israel in Mount Sinai.

2. The Copulative *and* is often omitted; as *Արձրկեցէք՝ բերէք ինծի*, Loose them and bring them to me. (Matt. 21 : 2.)

' 3 Adjectives are formed from Prepositions by the addition of *ի*; as *վրայ* upon, *վրայի* which is upon, *ներս* within, *ներսի* that which is within, internal.

4. Proper names when transferred from Greek to Armenian change β into *բ*; as Ἀβραάμ, *Աբրահամ*; γ into *գ*, as Γαλιλαία, *Գալիլեայ*; δ into *դ*, as Ἰούδας, *Ուդայ*; θ into *թ*, as Ῥοίθ, *Հռութ*; ι initial when followed by a vowel into *յ*, as Ἰησοῦς, *Յիսուս*; κ into *կ*, as Ἰσαάκ, *Իսահակ*; λ frequently into *ղ*, as Σολομὼν, *Սողոմոն*; π into *պ* and τ into *տ*, as Πέτρος, *Պետրոս*; φ into *փ*, as Φίλιππος, *Փիլիպպոս*; and χ into *ք*, as Χριστὸς, *Քրիստոս*: It is worthy of remark that these letters without exception occupy corresponding places in the respective alphabets. Besides, *բ* is sometimes, especially in the East, pronounced as *b*, *գ* as *g* hard, *դ* as *d*. This pronunciation is now esteemed vulgar. Still its existence, together with the usage pointed out above, seems to indicate that a considerable change has taken place in the pronunciation of the Armenian letters.

5. The spoken Armenian has, in common with the Turkish, the singular usage of repeating nouns and adjectives (and occasionally other parts of speech) substituting in the repetition a *մ* for the first letter of the word if it begin with a consonant, and prefixing a

Մ if it begin with a vowel, for the purpose sf *gene-ralizing* the idea contained in the word so repeated; thus Գիրք միրք փնտռեցի չգտայ, *I sought for books or any thing of the kind, but found none*; Խանութ մանութ չմնաց · բոլորը այրունեցաւ, *Not a shop or any thing like one remains, every thing has been burnt*; Ձռնած տունդ ջոր մոր չունի՞, *Has the house which you have taken no well, cistern, fountain, &c?* Հաց բեր՝ չոր մոր ըլլայ, *Bring bread, no matter if it be somewhat dry or crumbled.* Sometimes an ու appears between the two forms; as ծուռ ու մուռ *zigzag, serpentine*, սուտ ու մուտ *crafty, wily.* When a word commences with մ the same result is sometimes produced by changing a vowel; as Մազ մուզ չմնաց, *Not a hair nor any thing like one was left*, Մանր մունր (vulg. մանոր մունոր) բաներ, *Litle trifling matters.*

6. Sometimes ր takes the place of լ in colloquial language; Չեմ կրնար բերեր, *I cannot bring.* Somewhat resembling this are such expressions also as չկրցայ բերեր էի, չկրցանք բերեր էինք, which have perhaps originated in combining the two ideas *could not bring* and *would have brought*, q. d. բերեր էի (in the sense of պիտի բերէի) բայց չկրցայ ·

7. Though the Armenian language, etymologically considered, appears to stand by itself, having no such close relation to any other language of the great Indo-European family as the French has, for instance, with the Italian, or the Bulgarian with the Russian, &c. still its vocabulary exhibits some resemblances to other languages, both Asiatic and European, which are deserving of notice. The following may serve as Specimens.

HEBREW AND COGNATE DIALECTS.

Կ․ատատ , Heb. *kodkod*, crown, summit.

Ծ․ո՛հ , Heb. *zevakh*, sacrifice.

Հաշիւ , a reckoning, Heb. *khashav*, to reckon.

Ծոմ , Heb. *tsum*, fasting.

Ծրար , Heb. *tseror*, a bundle.

Մաքս , Heb. *mekes*, tribute.

Շուշան , Heb. *shushan*, a lily.

Ոժ , Heb. *oz*, strength.

Սիւն, a column, Heb. *tsiun*, a monument.

Չամաք , dry land, Heb. *tsamak*, to be dry.

Քահանայ, Heb. *kohen*, Chald. (emph. st.) *kahana*, a priest.

Քարոզ , Chald. *karoz*, a herald.

Քուրմ , Heb. Plur. *kemarim*, Syr. *koomar*, an idolatrous priest.

Ազատ , Pers. *azad*, free.

Զէթ , Arab. *zeit*, olive oil.

Նշան , Pers. *nishan*, a sign.

Տրտում , sad, Pers. *derd*, sadness.

Ուխտ , Arab. *akhd*, covenant.

GREEK AND LATIN.

Անկիւն , ἀγκών, a corner.

Աստղ , ἀστήρ, a star.

Ծոյգ , ζεῦγος, a yoke, a pair.

Լոյս , *lux*, light.

Կին , γυνή, a woman, a wife.

Մայր , μήτηο, *mater*, mother.

Յորդորել , *hortor*, to exhort.

Նաւ , ναῦς, *navis*, a ship.

Պնակ ; πινάκιον, a plate.

Պոռնիկ , πόρνη, a harlot.

Սերմ , semen, seed.

Տամ ; δίδωμι, do, to give.

Րոպէ , ῥοπή, an instant.

ENGLISH (AND COGNATE MODERN DIALECTS.)

Դառնալ , to turn.

Դուռ , door.

Լափել , to lap.

Կառք , carriage, car.

Կատու , cat.

Կով , cow.

Միս , meat.

Հերա , shred.

Ո՞, Ո՞վ , who ?

Ոտն , foot.

Վատ , bad.

Փունջ , bunch.

The introduction of such words as եկեղեցի , ἐκκλησία, կանոն , κανὼν, հեթանոս , ἔθνος, հերետիկոս , αἱρετικὸς, &c. after the introduction of christianity, is easy to be accounted for, and implies nothing whatever in regard to the original structure and relations of the language.

SALUTATIONS.

On meeting in the morning, Բարի լոյս , *Good morning!* the answer to which is Աստուծոյ բարին , *The blessing of God!*

In the middle of the day Բարեւ , or Բարեւ ձեզի , or Բարով is sometimes employed when in English we shuld still say *Good morning!* The answer is the same as above.

On meeting in the evening Բարի իրիկուն , *Good evening!* Reply as above.

At parting, the person who leaves says, Մնաք բա~

բով or Կեցի՛ք բարով , the reply to which is Երթա՛ք
բարով , both answering to our *Good by*, or *Farewell*.

On separating in the evening Գիշեր բարի , or Բարի
գիշեր , *Good night*. Answer Բեղ լյս բարի , which
extends the idea of the salutation to the morning
light.

Returning after an absence one is greeted with
Բարի (or բարով) եկար (or եկաք) , *Welcome* ! to which
he replies Բարով տեսանք , which may be rendered,
I am happy to see you. If the newcomer has entered the
room in the absence of the person whom he comes
to visit, the latter on coming in makes use of the
same salutation only substituting the Perfect tense
for the Aorist, thus Բարի եկեր ես , or բարի ես եկեր .

Give my compliments to . . . . is expressed by շատ
բարև ըրէ . . . . The person who is to convey
them assumes the responsibility by saying Գլխուս
վրայ , and acquits himself of it, when he meets the
person to whom the greetings are sent, by saying,
. . . ձեզի շատ բարև կ'ընէ (or ունի) to which the other
replies Շնորհակալ եմ , *Thank you*, or Իրկոզ թերոզը
ողջ կենայ (or մնայ) , as we say, *I am much obliged both
to you and to him*.

At the beginning of the new year Շնոր հաւոր նոր
տարի , *A happy new year*. Also Աստուած շատ տարի-
ներու հասցունէ . Ամէն տարի բարով հանիք , (or more
learnedly) Ամէն տարի բարեաւ խաղաղութեամբ , which
phrases are also used in saluting a person on his
anniversary festival, i. e. the day of the Saint whose
name he bears.

At Christmas (January 6) in like manner, Շնոր-
հաւոր ծնունդ , or, in some places, Քրիստոս ծնաւ և

Յայտնեցաւ , to which one may answer, Օրհնեալ է ծնունդ և յայտնութիւնն Քրիստոսի , alluding to the fact that the festival of the *Manifestation* (i. e. E-piphany) and Christmas are both celebrated on the same day.

At Easter and for forty days after Քրիստոս յարեաւ 'ի մեռելոց *Christ is risen from the dead* Answer, Օրհնեալ է յարութիւնն Քրիստոսի . *Blessed be the resurrection of Christ.*

Beside the above, which are for set times, there is a great variety of occasional salutations, such as Աչքդ լոյս, *Light to your eyes*! addressed to one whose son or daughter has just been married, to parents on the birth of a child, or to those who have just welcomed a near relative or dear friend from abroad, or even received a letter from such a friend. The person to whom this salutation is addressed replies Լուսով կե-նաս , *May you enjoy the light* ! To one who enters a new dwelling the salutation is Բարով նստիս ; to one who puts on a new garment, Բարով հինցընես ; to one who is commencing an enterprise, Աստուած յաջողու-թիւն տայ ; to one who is convalescing after an illness, Անցաւոր ըլլայ ; to one who has lost a friend, Քեզի օրիր or Գլուխդ ողջ մնայ . The phrase Օրերդ շատ ըլլայ is often used in the same sense with Շնոր-հակալ եմ , *Thank you.* So also is Ապրիս , especially when addressed to child or an inferior.

MISCELLANEOUS IDIOMATIC PHRASES.

Օախու առած գիրքս ։	The book which I bought.
Իր բնակած տունը ։	The house in which he lives.

Եղած ատենը ։	The time when it was done.
Գտնուած տեղը ։	The place where it was found.
Առած տեղդ դիր ։	Put it in the place from which you took it.
Ուզածս աս է ։	This is what I wished.
Կրցածիդ չափի բրէ ։ } Չեւքեդ եկածին չափի բրէ ։ }	Do as much as you can.
Բրածը չգիտեր ։	He does not know what he is about.
Հոն հասնելուդ պէս նամակ դրէ ։	Write immediately on your arrival there.
Ժամացոյցս առաջ կ'երթայ ։	My watch goes too fast.
Երբեմն քիչ մը ետ կը մնայ ։	Sometimes it loses a little.
Կայնած է ։	It has stopped.
Լարէ ուրեմն , (*խուրմիշ բրէ) ։	Wind it up then.
Կօշիկներս տար շինել տուր ։	Take my boots and get them mended.
Շաբաթը երկու անգամ կու գայ ։	He comes twice a week.
Երկու օրը անգամ մը ։	Once in two days.
Հիմա կու գայ ։	He will be here presently.
Հիմա գնաց ։	He has just gone.
Հիւանդը ինտո՞ր է ։	How is the sick man ?
Ինտոր եր նէ՛ անանկ է ։	He is the same as he was.
Երեկուան պէս աղէկ չէ ։	He is not so well as he was yesterday.

*Turkish words. See Preface.

Հիմա առաջուրնէ՛ *տաՀա ադեկ է :	He is now better than he was.
Ո՛ր թժիշկը կրնայի :	What Doctor attends him ?
Ձիւնի պէս ճերմակ է :	It is as white as snow.
Եղբօրմէս մեծ եմ ․	I am older than my bro- ther.
Մ՛եկիկ մեկիկ դուրս Հանէ :	Take them out one by one.
Երկերկու Հատ :	Two at a time.
Իրեք իրեք Հատ :	There at a time.
Հարիւրական *փարա :	A hundred paras apiece .
Շատոնց է որ քեզ տեսած չունիմ :	It is a long time since I have seen you.
Կը բերէի կոր , բայց չեղաւ :	I would have brought it, but did not succeed.
Ես չըլլայի նէ՛ պիտի խեղդուէր :	But for my help he would have been drowned.
Մ՛աղ մնաց որ աչքս պիտի ելլէր :	I came within a hair's breadth of having my eye put out.
Քիչ մնաց որ աչքէ մը պիտի ըներ զիս :	He came very near caus- ing me the loss of an eye.
Սիրաս մի՛ (or մը) նեղացուներ :	Do not trouble me.
Ատիկայ ճերք տուաւ ․	That was sufficient.
Ինծի ճերք չառ :	I cannot afford it.
Ձերք ըրաւ ինծի :	He beckoned to me.
Աչք ըրաւ անոր ։	He winked at him.
Խելքը դլուխը եկաւ :	He came to his senses.
Դլուխը նեղն դայուն պէս : Դլուխը քարին եկաւ նէ : }	When he got into trouble.

10

Ազնիւ բնաւորութեան տէր մարդ մըն է :	He has a noble disposition.
Նանի տեղ չի (or չ) դներ անիկայ :	He regards that as of no account.
Երեսպաշտութիւն կընէ անոր :	He makes court to him.
Սիրտս եա կու գայ :	I am sick at my stomach.
Սիրտս կ՚առնէ :	I cannot eat it (on account of the sweetness or oiliness of the food).
Սիրտս կը մարի :	I am faint.
Շատ առնելիք ունիմ :	I have much due me.
Շուտով կ՚առնուի :	He is easily touched.
Երեսը կախ է :	He has a sullen look.
Երեսէն *զէշիր [թոյն] կը կաթէ :	He is cross—he frowns.
Եթէ որ ինքզինքդ սիրցունես նէ՝ ձեռքի վրայ կը թռնեն քեզ :	If you try to please them they will do well by you.
Ո՜ւր էր որ ասանկ ըլլար :	Oh that it might be so!
Գլխու վրայ կը թռնեի անիկայ :	I paid him much honor.
Ժանիքը կախեր է :	He is out of humor.
Ծուծի ժանիք կ՚ընէ :	He looks awry at me.
Ո՛չ ուտելը գիտէ՝ ո՛չ պահելը :	He knows neither how to spend nor how to keep.
Ամէն ունեցածը մազի վրայ է :	His all is at stake.
Հասցէն գրէ :	Address the letter.
Միտքս եկաւ :	It occured to me.
Միտքը ձգէ անիկայ .	Remind him of it.
Ի սածներս մի՛ տրդ պաշէ :	Remember what I say.

Ամենուն մէյմէկ հատ տաս։	Give one to each of them.
Բովս մտաւ։	He entered my service.
Դիխուն գալ։	To happen to any one.
Դլուխը պիտի չհանեն անի֊ կայ։	They will not accomplish it.
Հունչը կտրեցաւ։	He was out of breath.
Քունս աչքս կը վազէ։	I am very drowsy.
Դլուն 'ի վար գնաց։	It went down head fore-most.
Կիտես թէ ոտքին տակը հաւկիթ կայ։	He walks as softly as if he were treading upon eggs.
Վախուն սիրտը փրթաւ։	He was overcome with fear.
Լեղիս կը պատոէր կոր։	It alarms me excessively.
Յնալ մը ինկայ որ չորս դիս կոտրեցաւ։	I fell down and hurt my-self all over.
Վրադ գլուխդ փոխէ։	Change your clothes.
Ձիէն ալ անցաւ։	He outran the horse.
Մէկ զարնելուն մեռցուց։	He killed him at one blow.
Ինք իր գլխուն ըրաւ (մե֊ կուն չհարցուցած)։	He did it of his own ac-cord (without consulting any one.)
Այս մտոք առնուած։	Understood in this sense.
Խօսք բացինք։	We commenced conversa-tion.
Խօսքի մէջ մտնալ։	To interrupt conversation.
Որչափի (or ի՞նչ *խատը) կը քշէ։	How long will it take?
Աց մը փրցուց։	He broke out crying.
Խօսքին վրայ կը կենայ։	He stands to his word.
Աւիկայ բանի մը չի գար։	This is good for nothing.

Ա՛չք անցուր :	Cast your eye over it.
Ասանկ գիրք ձեռքս անցած չունէր :	Such a book I had never seen.
Ուտելու կուգայ , բայց պահելու չիգար :	It is good to eat, but will not do to keep.
Թարթիչները ճերմակի կը պռնեն :	His eye-lashes incline to white.
Անոր մորթը կարմիրի կը չալէ :	Its skin is reddish.
*Հ՛աւա բրաւ .	He did it in jest.
Երկու *խաթ բրէ ՛պիճմը :	Double the string.
Տունը երկու ՛խաթ է :	The house is two stories high.
Խոսք կապը տուին :	They have given a token.
Գիրքին վրան բան մը անցուր :	Put a cover on the book.
Անկից հոն՛ անկից հոն՛ ի՞նչ պիտի րլլայ :	Why move it about from place to place ?
Ո՛ւր է աս՛ ուր է ան :	What comparison is there between this and that ?
Վանը ձունը չելաւ :	Nothing has transpired respecting it.
Մ՛խտը բաց տղայ է :	He is a bright boy.
Մ՛խտը գոց տղայ է :	He is a dull boy.
Վիթը անկից :	He was offended.
Վիթ չիշրեր :	He will not condescend to such a trifle.
Վիթը կախեր է :	He is drooping.
Ականջ չկախեր	He does not give ear.
Հիւանդ է եղեր :	He is sick (i. e. it is reported or is is understood that he is sick.)

Թագաւորը Հրաման ըրեր է եղեր որ սպաննուի :	It is understood that the king has given orders for his execution.
Պղտիկ լեռները ան է սաղձ֊ ծեր․	He boasts as if he could create a world.
Լեզուն քիչ մը կարճցաւ :	His talk has moderated a little.
Բարը տեղը դրաւ․	He has hit the nail on the head.
Կարը կարկուտքը պակաս չէ :	He is alway tinkering.
Օուլ կարեցաւ :	It was flooded, overflowed.
Չուր կարեցայ մնացի․	I stood still in amazement.
Սարյես լեռ մը եղաւ :	I was relieved of a mountain's weight.
Ունելիքս չմաց : Էլ ընելիք չունիմ	I have no resource left.
*Թօփ նետեց (Սնանկա֊ ցաւ) :	He has become bankrupt.
Ներանս վրայ չերթար : Լեզուս վրայ չերթար :	I cannot bear to speak (on so painful a subject.)
Ձեռքը երկան է :	He is thievish.
Ի՞նչ ընեմ ձեռքս կարճ է :	What can I do ? I have not the means.
Ձեռքս չհասաւ :	I did not succeed.
Նասնկ մարդուն խնէք տուիր :	Would you notice such a man ?
Ես քու խելքդ գլուխդ կը բերեմ :	I'll bring you to your senses.
Սատկի խենթ , այրանքի խենթ :	Crazy after money, or property.
Ունեցածը չունեցածը ձա֊	He has been obliged to

խեց ։	sell every thing.
Տակր փախուց ։	He has wasted his capital.
Ասանկ անձրևով ի՞նչպես երթալ կուզէ ։	How can one go in such a rain ?
Ի՞նչ ըսել կուզէ ատ խոսքր ։	What is the meaning of that word ?
Դլուխս իմս չէ ։	I am crazy with a head-ache.
Մէջքս չըռներ կոր ։	My back is almost broken (with aching from a cold.)
Մազերս փուշ փուշ եղաւ ։	My hair stood on end.
Տակաւին լեզուն չդառնար ։	He does not begin to talk. (Spoken of an in-fant.)
Մատերս կր փատնան ։	My fingers are numb.
Ձեռքս փրթաւ՝ մինչև հոս բերելս ։	It broke my hand off to bring it— I brought it with great difficulty.
Պուն ինչ ես նէ՝ ես ալ ան եմ ։	I have equal claims with you.
Աչք կրնէ որ չըսեմ, բայց ոʼվ ականջ կր կախէ ։	He beckons to me not to speak, but who cares ?
Մարդ կայ՝ մարդ ալ կայ ։	There are more sorts of men than one.
Յոգին հանեց ։	He wearied him out.
Դլուխս կր տանէր կոր , ես ալ տուի ։	He teazed me so much. that I gave it to him.
Տակր կրան մէկ է ։	The outside and the inside are the same. (Spoken of cloth.)

Տակն ու վրայ ըրաւ մեզի : He has put us all in confu-
sion.

Տունըրնիդ կրուեցա՞ք : Have you moved to your
house.

Նեղ օրիդ քեզի հասնողը Who rendered you aid
ով էր : when you were in want ?

Ինչերը հերիք խառնես : Don't dwell on former
troubles.

Ատ լսելուս սիրաս եկաւ : I was overcome on hear-
ing it.

Մեղք է ինձի : I an to be pitied.
Մեղք չե՞մ ես : Am I not to be pitied¨?
Խօսքս ամօթ . . . Pardon the expression . . .
Ատ ի՞նչ կըսես՝ հիմա խելքս What do you say ? I shall
կը թռցունեմ : lose my senses.

Չայնդ կտրէ : Be quiet.

Անիկայ ձեռքը բաց մարդ He is a liberal man.
մ'է :

Սիրտը մեծ մարդ է : He is proud man.

Ետքը գլխուն շատ պիտի He will be very sorry for
դարնէ : it hereafter.

Ինձի՞ ալ գլխէ պիտի հա- Will you lead me also a-
նես : stray ?

Քեզի համար տունէ մը ե- For your sake (or by your
ղայ : means) I have lost a
house.

Տունս տեղս փլցուց : He has lost me all my
property.

Գնա ՛ սեւերես մնացիր : Go, and shame on you !
Աչքի եկաւ : He has been affectcd by an
evil eye—is bewitched.

Ꮑեռը մարդ կարերկ է ։ The hill is full of people.

Փատցաւ մնաց ։ He stood stock still.

Քար կարեցաւ ։ He became like a stone.

Քարը կը խօսի նէ՝ ան ալ խօսեցաւ . He was as still as a stone.

Դլուխը քարը ։ I have done with the good-for-nothing fellow. Let him do what he likes.

Ꮑերնատունը մարդ չկայ ։ He is weak in the upper story.

Դլուխը կերաւ . He was the cause of his death

Յաւ ու ցեցը պակաս չէ ։ Always ailing.

Սիրտդ լայն բունէ ։ Be patient.

Դանես գործես եղայ ։ I was hindered in my work.

Մ՚իաս ի՞նչ կը ծամես ։ Why do you slander me ?

Խելքը դլուխը մարդ մըն է ։ He is a prudent man.

Խելքը միտքը խաղալ է ։ His whole heart and soul is upon play.

Խելք դլուխ ժողվէ ։ Learn wisdom, or come to your senses.

Խելքդ վրադ պահէ որ քեր . Do not suffer yourself to be overcome with grief.

Խելքս չկարեր ։ I can not understand.

Ꮑնգեր մնացեր է ։ He has become a dotard.

Տեսածիս պես խելքս դլնես թռաւ ։ When I saw it I was overcome (with grief, fear, or astonishment).

Մ՚աղը ծակ է ։ Take care, your are overheard.

Հատ ու բարակ մէկ՚ դին է։ It is of no use to be too nice. People will not notice the difference.

Հոգիդ կելլա՞ր կոր ։ Were you dying, that you were in such a hurry?

Լեզուին տալ ։ To talk at random.

Լեզուն օսկոր չունի ։ He talks without restraint.

Լեզուն երկան է . He talks much.

Լեզու թափել ։ To talk fluently.

Քիթդ մեծցեր է ։ You have grown proud.

Քիթը իջեցուցի ։ I humbled his pride.

Մ'նշ եղաւ եղաւ ։ Forget the past.

Մ'որ տուի անոր ։ I *gave it to* him. (Spoken of rebukes or threats.)

Մ'րատ ծակեց նէ' ինառր չխօսիմ ։ He affronted me so, how could I help speaking?

Չ'ենմ լանք Չ'ենմ երթանք ։ We must not stop too long for unessential things.

Կայր երթայը մէկ եղաւ . He came and went immediately.

Բրաւ չըրաւ միտքս պառեցուց ։ By various means he persuaded me.

Ինչո՞ւ կուիլ կը շանես ։ Why do you become the occasion of strife?

Երեսի կեղտ ես ողեր ։ You have dishonored your family.

Մարձրեն մի' թոիր ։ Do not venture too far, nor boastingly promise more than you can perform.

Երեսը թթուեցուց ։ He is out of humor.

11

Եկո՛ւր երեսս ընենք ։	Come, let us look into the matter with the parties concerned.
Ներան եկեր է ։	He is of proper age.
Զերքը թերանը չՀատած կը կարգեն ։	They marry (their children) before they are fit to provide for themselves.
Խնքես կերթար որ դեշու թիւն չբառվի ։	I tried with all my might to prevent him from learning wickedness.
*Ինչ մ՚ Հարցուներ ։	I cannot tell (how badly matters are going).
Անոր խելքը կերթայ կու գայ ։	He is unstable.
Դլխու ցաւ ես եղեր ։	You distract me with your teazing.
Անանջը ծակ մարդ է ։	He is a man of quick apprehension.
Ասանկ աչքը ծակ տեսած չեմ ։	I never saw such an insatiable person.
Սիրտը առնել ։	To appease, to tranquilize.
Երեսի ջուր չունի ։	He has no shame.
Երեսի ջուրը կորանցուցեր է ։	He has lost all shame.
Երես տալ, երես Հանել ։	To encourage another to be free with you.
Երես եղեր է ։	He has become too bold and familiar.
Երեսը ձերմակ է ։	(Ironically) In disgrace.
Ասնի մը տեղ չներ ասիկայ ։	He does not value this.
Ժամը քանի՞ է ։	What o'clock is it ?
Ութն է ։	It is eight.
Ժամը ութնին եկաւ ։	He came at eight o'clock.

ABBREVIATIONS.

Ա՛ծ	or	ած	for	Աստուած		God
Ա՛յ	or	այ	,,	Աստուծոյ		of God
Ա՛վ	or	աւ	,,	Աստուծով		with God's help
Յս			,,	Յիսուս		Jesus
Յսի	or	Յի	,,	Յիսուսի		of Jesus
Քս			,,	Քրիստոս		Christ
Քսի	or	Քի	,,	Քրիստոսի		of Christ
Տր			,,	Տէր		Lord
ամ			,,	ամենայն or ամէն		all
թի	or	ի	,,	թիւն	}	
թե	or	ե	,,	թեան	} terminations	
թր	or	ր	,,	թեամբ	}	
կմ	or	կ	,,	կամ		or
որպ			,,	որպէս		as
պս	or	պ	,,	պէս		like
սրբ			,,	սուրբ		holy
վրյ	or	վր	,,	վրայ		upon
քն	or	ք	,,	քան		than
այ			,,	այսինքն		namely
օր			,,	զոր օրինակ		for example
ընդ			,,	ընդ		with, by, &c.
ըստ			,,	ըստ		according to
և			,,	եայլն		and so forth

APPENDIX.

Besides the irregularities mentioned on pp. 13—17, forms of nouns not unfrequently appear in the modern language derived from the ancient declensions. As no precise limit can be assigned to the introduction of such forms, it has been thought worth while to append here a synoptical table of the declensions of ancient nouns, premising a few brief and general rules for the formation of the cases.

The declensions are generally reckoned ten. Different grammarians however group them differently, and the tenth is little else than a collection of heteroclites.

In the table the prefixed and suffixed formative letters, except in the tenth declension, are distinguished from the root by being printed in italics.

RULES FOR THE FORMATION OF THE CASES.

1. IN THE SINGULAR.

The *Genitive* has various endings which must be learned from the Lexicon. The most common are *ի* and *ոյ* .--But polysyllabic nouns in *ի* make the Genitive in *ւոյ* .

Nouns in *իւն* make the Genitive   in *եան*

  ,,   *ն* preceded by a consonant in *ին* or *ան*

  ,,   *ր*   ,,   ,,   in *եր*

Proper nouns for the most part make the Gen. in *այ* .

The *Dative* has two forms, one always the same with the Gen. the other the same with the Nom. with *՛ի* prefixed in case the noun begins with a consonant, and ⲩ or (rarely) 'ի ⲩ in case it begins with a vowel.

The *Accusative* is the Nom. with ⲍ prefixed.

The *Ablative* always prefixes 'ի or ⲩ like the second form of the Dative. Its termination is genarally է added to the form of the Nom.

But if the Gen. end in ⲟⲩ or ⲱⲩ․ the termination of the Abl. is the same.

Nouns which have the Gen. ending in ⲟⲩ, ⲱⲛ, ⲃⲣ, ⲟⲩ or other irregular terminations *add* է to the Genitive to form the Ablative.

Genitives in ⲃⲱⲛ make the Ablative in ⲃⲛէ ; those in իⲛ ․ in ⲱⲛէ ․

The *Narrative* * is the same as the Ablative, substituting a prefixed ⲍ for 'ի ․

The *Instrumental* depends upon the form of the Gen.

Genitives in		ի make the Instr. in		իⲩ or ⲱⲩ
,,		ⲟⲩ	,,	,,	ⲟⲩ
,,		ⲟⲩ	,,	,,	ⲃⲱⲩ or ⲟⲩ
,,	ⲱⲛ & իⲛ		,,	,,	ⲱⲙի
,,		ⲟⲩ	,,	,,	ⲟⲩ
,,		ⲱⲩ	,,	,,	ⲱⲩ
,,		ⲃⲣ	,,	,,	ⲃⲣⲣ
,,		ⲟⲣ	,,	,,	ⲱⲣⲣ

The *Circumlative* * is the same as the Instrumental with ⲍ prefixed.

The *Commorative* * has generally two forms, viz. those of the Nom. and Gen. with 'ի or ⲩ prefixed.

The *Vocative* is the same as the Nom. with or without the Interjection ⲟⲩ ․

*The force of the Narrative case may generally by expressed in English by the preposition *concerning*, that of the Circumlative by *around*, and that of the Commorative (or Locative) by *in*.

II. IN THE PLURAL.

The *Nominative Plural* always ends in _p_ and is formed generally by adding this letter to the Nom. Sing.

But nouns which have the Gen. Sing. in _ի_ , _եր_ , _ու_ or _այ_ add _p_ to that case to form the Nom. Plur.

And nouns ending in _այր_ make the Plur. in _արp_

The *Genitive Plural* always ends in _g_ .

If the Instr. Sing. have _իւ_ the Gen. Plur. has _իg_

,,	,,	,,	_աւ_	,,	,,	_աg_
,,	,,	,,	_ոյ_	,,	,,	_ոg_
,,	,,	,,	_ու_	,,	,,	_ուg_
,,	,,	,,	_ամբ_	,,	,,	_անg_
,,	,,	,,	_երբ_	,,	,,	_երg_
,,	,,	,,	_արբ_	,,	,,	_արg_ or _անարg_

The *Dative* as in the Sing. has two forms ; one like the Gen. and the other like the Acc. with _'ի_ or _ յ_ prefixed instead of _զ_ .

The *Accusative* is formed from the Nom. by prefixing _զ_ and changing the final _p_ into _ս_ .

The *Ablative* is formed from the Gen. by prefixing _'ի_ or _ յ_ .

The *Narrative* the same, substituting _զ_ for that prefix.

The *Instrumental* is formed from the Instr. Sing. by adding _p_ . But _աւ_ becomes _օp_ (in ancient mss. _աւp_).

The *Circumlative* from the Instr. by prefixing _զ_ .

The *Commorative* from the Acc. by prefixing _'ի_ or _ յ_ instead of _զ_ .

The *Vocative* (as in the Sing.) is like the Nom.

DECLENSION OF ANCIENT ARMENIAN NOUNS.

Dec. 1.　　Dec. 2.　　Dec. 3.　　Dec. 4.

Singular.

	Word	*City*	*River*	*Church*
Nom.	Բան	Քաղաք	Գետ	Եկեղեցի
Gen.	Բանի	Քաղաքի	Գետոյ	Եկեղեցւոյ
Dat.	Բանի / ՚ի Բան	Քաղաքի / ՚ի Քաղաք	Գետոյ / ՚ի Գետ	Եկեղեցւոյ / յեկեղեցի
Acc.	զԲան	զՔաղաք	զԳետ	զԵկեղեցի
Abl.	՚ի Բանէ	՚ի Քաղաքէ	՚ի Գետոյ	յեկեղեցւոյ
Nar.	զԲանէ	զՔաղաքէ	զԳետոյ	զԵկեղեցւոյ
Instr.	Բանիւ	Քաղաքաւ	Գետով	Եկեղեցեաւ
Circ.	զԲանիւ	զՔաղաքաւ	զԳետով	զԵկեղեցեաւ
Com.	՚ի Բանի / ՚ի Բան	՚ի Քաղաքի / ՚ի Քաղաք	՚ի Գետ	յեկեղեցւոջ / յեկեղեցի
Voc.	ո՜ Բան	ո՜ Քաղաք	ո՜ Գետ	ո՜ Եկեղեցի

Plural.

Nom.	Բանք	Քաղաքք	Գետք	Եկեղեցիք
Gen.	Բանից	Քաղաքաց	Գետոց	Եկեղեցեաց
Dat.	Բանից / ՚ի Բանս	Քաղաքաց / ՚ի Քաղաքս	Գետոց / ՚ի Գետս	Եկեղեցեաց / յեկեղեցիս
Acc.	զԲանս	զՔաղաքս	զԳետս	զԵկեղեցիս
Abl.	՚ի Բանից	՚ի Քաղաքաց	՚ի Գետոց	յեկեղեցեաց
Nar.	զԲանից	զՔաղաքաց	զԳետոց	զԵկեղեցեաց
Instr.	Բանիւ	Քաղաքաւ	Գետովք	Եկեղեցեաւք
Circ.	զԲանիւք	զՔաղաքաւք	զԳետովք	զԵկեղեցեաւք
Com.	՚ի Բանս	՚ի Քաղաքս	՚ի Գետս	յեկեղեցիս
Voc.	ո՜ Բանք	ո՜ Քաղաքք	ո՜ Գետք	ո՜ Եկեղեցիք

Dec. 5 a.   Dec. 5 b.   Dec. 6 a.   Dec. 6 b.

Singular.

	Hour	*Little*	*Foundation*	*Trouble*
Nom.	Ժամ	Փոքր	հիմն	Նեղութիւն
Gen.	Ժամու	Փոքու	հիման	Նեղութեան
Dat.	Ժամու / ՚ի Ժամ	Փոքու / ՚ի Փոքր	հիման / ՚ի հիմն	Նեղութեան / ՚ի Նեղութիւն
Acc.	զԺամ	զՓոքր	զհիմն	զՆեղութիւն
Abl.	՚ի Ժամէ	՚ի Փոքուէ	՚ի հիմանէ	՚ի Նեղութենէ
Nar.	զԺամէ	զՓոքուէ	զհիմանէ	զՆեղութենէ
Instr.	Ժամու	Փոքու	հիմամբ	Նեղութեամբ
Circ.	զԺամու	զՓոքու	զհիմամբ	զՆեղութեամբ
Com.	՚ի Ժամու / ՚ի Ժամ	՚ի Փոքու / ՚ի Փոքր	՚ի հիման / ՚ի հիմն	՚ի Նեղութեան / ՚ի Նեղութիւն
Voc.	ո՛վ Ժամ	ո՛վ Փոքր	ո՛վ հիմն	ո՛վ Նեղութիւն

Plural.

	Hour	*Little*	*Foundation*	*Trouble*
Nom.	Ժամք	Փոքունք	հիմունք	Նեղութիւնք
Gen.	Ժամուց	Փոքունց	հիմանց	Նեղութեանց
Dat.	Ժամուց / ՚ի Ժամու	Փոքունց / ՚ի Փոքունս	հիմանց / ՚ի հիմունս	Նեղութեանց / ՚ի Նեղութիւնս
Acc.	զԺամս	զՓոքունս	զհիմունս	զՆեղութիւնս
Abl.	՚ի Ժամուց	՚ի Փոքունց	՚ի հիմանց	՚ի Նեղութեանց
Nar.	զԺամուց	զՓոքունց	զհիմանց	զՆեղութեանց
Instr.	Ժամուք	Փոքունբք	հիմամբք	Նեղութեամբք
Circ.	զԺամուք	զՓոքունբք	զհիմամբք	զՆեղութեամբք
Com.	՚ի Ժամու	՚ի Փոքունս	՚ի հիմունս	՚ի Նեղութիւնս
Voc.	ո՛վ Ժամք	ո՛վ Փոքունք	ո՛վ հիմունք	ո՛վ Նեղութիւնք

	Dec. 7.	Dec. 8.	Dec. 9.
	Singular.		
	Lamb	*Bone*	*Adam*
Nom.	Գառն	Ոսկր	Ադամ
Gen.	Գառին	Ոսկեր	Ադամայ
Dat.	Գառին 'ի Գառն	Ոսկեր յՈսկր	Ադամայ յԱդամ
Acc.	զԳառն	զՈսկր	զԱդամ
Abl.	'ի Գառանէ	յՈսկերէ	յԱդամայ
Nar.	զԳառանէ	զՈսկերէ	զԱդամայ
Inst.	Գառամբ	Ոսկերբ	Ադամաւ
Circ.	զԳառամբ	զՈսկերբ	զԱդամաւ
Com.	'ի Գառին 'ի Գառն	յՈսկեր յՈսկր	յԱդամ
Voc.	ով Գառն	ով Ոսկր	ով Ադամ
	Plural.		
Nom.	Գառինք	Ոսկերք	
Gen.	Գառանց	Ոսկերց or ոսկերաց	
Dat.	Գառանց 'ի Գառինս	Ոսկերց or ոսկերաց յՈսկերս	
Acc.	զԳառինս	զՈսկերս	
Abl.	'ի Գառանց	յՈսկերց or յոսկերաց	
Nar.	զԳառանց	զՈսկերց or զոսկերաց	
Instr.	Գառամբք	Ոսկերբք or ոսկերօք	
Circ.	զԳառամբք	զՈսկերբք or զոսկերօք	
Com.	'ի Գառինս	յՈսկերս	
Voc.	ով Գառինք	ով Ոսկերք	

Dec. 10 a. Dec. 10 b. Dec. 10 c. Dec. 10 d.

Singular.

	Man	Father	Woman	Village
Nom.	այր	հայր	կին	գիւղ
Gen.	առն	հօր	կնոջ	գեղջ
Dat.	առն / ⸺ այր	հօր / ⸺ հայր	կնոջ / ⸺ կին	՚ի գեղջ / ՚ի գիւղ
Acc.	զայր	զհայր	զկին	զգիւղ
Abl.	յառնէ	՚ի հօրէ	՚ի կնոջէ	՚ի գեղջէ
Nar.	զառնէ	զհօրէ	զկնոջէ	զգեղջէ
Instr.	արամբ	հարբ	կանամբ / կնաւ	գիւղիւ
Circ.	զարամբ	զհարբ	զկանամբ / զկնաւ	զգիւղիւ
Com.	յառն / յայր	՚ի հօր / ՚ի հայր	՚ի կնոջ / ՚ի կին	՚ի գեղջ / ՚ի գիւղ
Voc.	ով այր	ով հայր	ով կին	ով գիւղ

Plural.

	Man	Father	Woman	Village
Nom.	արք	հարք	կանայք	գիւղք
Gen.	արանց	հարց / հարանց	կանանց	գիւղից
Dat.	արանց / ⸺ արս	հարց / հարանց / ⸺ հարս	կանանց / ⸺ կանայս	գիւղից / ՚ի գիւղս
Acc.	զարս	զհարս	զկանայս	զգիւղս
Abl.	յարանց	՚ի հարց / ՚ի հարանց	՚ի կանանց	՚ի գիւղից
Nar.	զարանց	զհարց / զհարանց	զկանանց	զգիւղից
Instr.	արամբք	հարբք	կանամբք	գիւղիւք
Circ.	զարամբք	զհարբք	զկանամբք	զգիւղիւք
Com.	յարս	՚ի հարս	՚ի կանայս	գիւղիւք
Voc.	ով արք	ով հարք	ով կանայք	ով գիւղք

COMPARATIVE SPECIMEN

Of Ancient Armenian, and of the Eastern and Western dialects of Modern Armenian.

PSALM I.

Ancient.

1 Երանեալ է այր որ ոչ գնաց 'ի խորհուրդս ամբարշտաց . 'ի ճանապարհս մեղաւորաց ոչ ո'չ եկաց, եւ յաթոռս ժանտից ո'չ նստաւ ։

2 Այլ յօրէնս Տեառն են կամք նորա, եւ յօրէնս նորա խորհեսցի նա 'ի տուէ եւ 'ի գիշերի ։

3 Եւ եղիցի նա որպէս ծառ, որ տնկեալ է 'ի գնացս ջուրց, որ զպտուղ իւր 'ի ժամու տացէ, եւ տերեւ նորա մի թափեսցի, եւ զամենայն զոր ինչ առնիցէ, յաջողեսցի նմա ։

4 Ո'չ այսպէս են ամբարիշտք, եւ ո'չ այնպէս . այլ որպէս փոշի, զոր հողմ հոսէ 'ի վերայ երեսաց երկրի ։

5 Վասն այնորիկ ո'չ յարիցեն ամբարիշտք 'ի դատաստան, եւ ոչ մեղաւորք 'ի խորհուրդս արդարոց ։

6 Քանզի ճանաչէ Տէր զճանապարհս արդարոց . ճանապարհ ամբարշտաց կորիցին ։

Modern Western.

1 Երանի՜ ան մարդուն` որ ամբարիշտներուն խորհուրդը չերթար, ու մեղաւորներուն ճամբան մէջ չկենար, ու ծաղր ընողներուն նստած տեղը չնստիր ։

2 Հապա անոր կամքը Տատուծոյ օրէնքին մէջն է . ու գիշեր ցորեկ անոր օրէնքին վրայ կը մտածէ ։

3 Եւ պիտի ըլլայ անիկայ ջուրերուն գնացքներքը տնկուած ծառի մը պէս, որ ժամանակին իր պտուղը կու տայ. ու անոր տերեքը չթափ ըլրնար, եւ ինչ բան որ ընէ` պիտի յաջողուի ։

4 Ըստանկ չեն ամբարիշտները . հապա մղեղին պէս, որ կը ցրուէ հովը ։

5 Ասոր համար ամբարիշտները դատաստանին կայներու չեն . ու ոչ մեղաւորները արդարներուն ժողովքին մէջ ։

6 Վասն զի Տէրը կը ճանչնայ արդարներուն ճամբան . բայց ամբարիշտներուն ճամբան պիտի կորսուի ։

Modern Eastern.

1 Երանելի՜ է են մարդըն` որ ամբարիշտներքի խորհըրդին մէջ չի գնում, եւ մեղաւորների ճանապարհին վերայ չի կանգնում, եւ չար ծաղրածողների աթոռին վերայ չի նստում ։

2 Այլ նորա կամքն` Տէրի օրէնքի միջումն է եւ ցերեկ եւ գիշեր նորա օրէնքին վերայ է մտածում ։

3 Եւ նա' է ինչպէս` ջրերի գնացքումն տնկուած ծառ` որ իրան պտուղն տալիս է իրան ժամանակումն եւ նորա տերեն չի վերթափվում, եւ ամէն ինչ որ անում է, յաջողվումէ նորան ։

4 Չըսպէս չեն ամբարիշտներն, այլ ինչպէս դարմանի մղեղ` որ քամին ցրիւ է տալիս նորան ։

5 Սրա համար ամբարիշտներն չեն վերկենալ դատաստանի մէջն եւ ոչ մեղաւորներն արդարների ժողովարդի մէջ ։

6 Պատճառն որ Տէրն ճանաչումէ արդարների ճանապարհն . իսկ ամբարիշտների ճանապարհն կը կորչի ։

INDEX.

Lightning Source UK Ltd.
Milton Keynes UK
UKOW011920271112

202880UK00009B/1112/P

9 781149 467619